Peter H. Kolvenbach
MEN OF GOD: MEN FOR OTHERS

Peter H. Kolvenbach
MEN OF GOD:
MEN FOR OTHERS

Peter-Hans Kolvenbach, SJ
Superior General of the Jesuits
interviewed by Renzo Giacomelli

Foreword by Vincent T. O'Keefe, SJ

Translated by Alan Neame

ALBA · HOUSE   NEW YORK

SOCIETY OF ST. PAUL, 2187 VICTORY BLVD., STATEN ISLAND, NEW YORK 10314

Original title: *Fedeli a Dio e all'uomo*
© 1990 Edizioni Paoline, s.r.l., Cinisello Balsamo (Milano), Italy

ISBN:0-8189-0600-6

Designed and produced by the Society of St. Paul,
an international congregation of religious men serving the Church
with the communications media.

Printing Information:

Current Printing - first digit   1   2   3   4   5   6   7   8   9   10   11   12

Year of Current Printing - first year shown
1990   1991   1992   1993   1994   1995   1996   1997

CONTENTS

FOREWORD ix

INTRODUCTION: WHO ARE THE JESUITS? xiii

    Six typical Jesuits xiii
    The founder xiv
    Persecuted and oppressed xvi
    Rebirth xviii
    The post-Conciliar tempest xix
    The Calvary of Father Arrupe xx
    A linguist in command of the Society xxi

1. IGNATIUS' EXAMPLE 3

    A "jubilee" for the Jesuits 3
    Ignatian discernment 4
    Ignatius as son of Rome 6
    Present-day value of the Spiritual Exercises 9
    Apostles before all else 12

2. JOYS AND SORROWS OF THE SOCIETY 17

    Growing apostolic commitment 17
    Ten thousand Jesuits fewer 20
    Crisis over lay brothers 23
    The contribution of the Third World 26
    Jesuit martyrs 28

3. THE POPE AND THE JESUITS 31

    Back to normality 31
    "The Jesuits" — a novel 33

The fourth vow is not discriminatory 34
The Church is not a parliament 40
Limited calls to order 42
To live the Council requires a change of heart 44
Communication between the Holy See and the Society 48

4. A SOCIETY OF MISSIONARIES 51

Evangelization and respect for other cultures 51
The mission in Africa 52
Asia: dialogue between religions 55
Latin America: siding with the poor 59
Liberation theology 61
Five centuries of Christianity in Latin America 64

5. POOR APOSTLES AND PROMOTERS OF JUSTICE 67

Poverty for the mission 67
No to political or trade union militancy 68
The whole Society for the promotion of justice 73
The difficult role of the Social Centers 76
The Jesuits and Italian politics 79

6. TEACHERS OF LIBERATION 83

A thousand schools of higher education 83
Promoters of justice or defenders of the "status quo"? 85
Obstacles to Catholic education 87
Pastoral activity and schooling 90
We shall never give up teaching 92
The Ignatian method of teaching 94
Jesuits and the mass media 96

7. NEW COMMITMENTS 101

In the Church and in the world 101
Religious indifference and atheism 102
The Society of Jesus in Eastern Europe 105
The difficulties of dialogue with Islam 110
Ecumenical dialogue is not marking time 114

8. THE CHALLENGES OF THE MODERN WORLD 119

Secularization and its ambiguities 119
Human values are not sufficient in themselves 121
Ecological and pacifist movements 124
"Global village" and public opinion 127
"Giving Europe a soul" 129
Restoring the balance between North and South 132
Towards the third millennium........................ 135

9. IN THE COMMUNITY OF BELIEVERS 137

The Jesuits in the local Churches 137
"Roman centralism" and the nomination of bishops........ 141
Moral theology, a minefield 144
No replacements for Rahner and de Lubac 145
The Society and the new movements within the Church 148
Relations with Opus Dei 150

10. COMMITTED TO THE PRESENT,
     WITNESSING TO THE FUTURE 153

The position of religious in the Church.................. 153
Religious life: "sign," not "model" 156
The ecclesial significance of religious vows 159
Religious life in human society 163

11. AN EXACTING TRAINING FOR ARDUOUS TASKS 167

Birth of a vocation 167
The period of studies 169
Priests when over thirty.............................. 171
Assessment of candidates 173
The apostolate dictates the destination 175

APPENDIX: CHRONOLOGY OF THE SOCIETY OF JESUS... 179

FOREWORD

Books by Jesuits as well as books about Jesuits are not an unusual event in the publishing world. But a book about the Jesuits by their Superior General, and in English to boot, is rather unusual.

Father Peter-Hans Kolvenbach, a Dutchman with 25 years of experience in the Middle East, was elected head of the Society of Jesus in 1983. Since then he has travelled all over the world to meet his brother Jesuits, and has also grown very familiar with the Roman scene. He is the most authoritative spokesman there is for the Society of Jesus.

Men of God: Men for Others is the result of an extended interview with a veteran Italian journalist, Renzo Giacomelli. He is an ideal interviewer because of his vast experience in ecclesial and religious matters, because his questions touch important and sensitive issues, and because he is tenacious in seeking answers to his questions.

In his replies, Father Kolvenbach is honest, frank and direct. This is his style. He is neither pat nor verbose in his answers, and the range of topics covered, shows his great breadth of knowledge along with an attention to detail where needed. There are some good insights into Church and Jesuit matters, and an occasional touch of humor so that the book does not run the risk of becoming what a friend describes as "terminally earnest."

Giacomelli's introduction and the interview itself provide a good account of the history of St. Ignatius of Loyola, of the Society he founded, its works today and of the 28th successor of St. Ignatius, Father Peter-Hans Kolvenbach.

A quick look at the topics treated shows we are dealing with substantial issues in the Church and world of today. Religious life treats vocations, their decrease or increase in certain parts of the world, the vows of religion and their relevance for today, how religious priests and brothers are educated and formed today, and the place of religious in the Church today.

The mission of all Jesuits today, defined by the last three General Congregations of the order as the service of faith and the promotion of justice in the name of the Gospel, is explored in different countries of the world, especially where it has been misunderstood and has caused problems and hostility and deaths, and also in the different works and ministries of the Jesuits, including the great number of educational institutions which they sponsor.

Relations with recent Popes are discussed, including the difficult period after Vatican II, and the years 1981-1983 when Pope John Paul II named his own personal delegate to govern the Society. Since 1983 relations have been peaceful and harmonious.

Certain tasks just opening up for the Society receive a full treatment, especially the situation in Central and Eastern Europe. Relations with socialist countries such as Cuba, and with communist countries such as China are discussed.

The interview brings to the fore many sensitive and controversial themes. These include: the relations between theologians and the teaching authority of the Church, and some specific cases are mentioned; the understanding and use of liberation theology; the accusation of Marxism leveled against some Jesuits; Jesuits and politics; ecological and pacifist movements; relations with new religious communities or movements such as Opus Dei; and the naming of bishops and "Roman centralism." This should give some idea of the lively issues which make up the interview.

Since it does discuss real issues and problems, and does present an authoritative spokesman to discuss them, the present volume is most welcome. It helps to put the book of Malachi Martin on the Jesuits in its proper place. For Father Kolvenbach its proper place is that of fiction and the novel rather than of serious history. Martin would have Father Kolvenbach speaking with people that the Jesuit General has never met in his whole life.

Men of God: Men for Others gives us a good look at what Jesuits are engaged in around the world and what they are trying to accomplish. It also tells us who they are and what leads them to the type of life they lead.

The present volume would be timely at any time, but its appearance now could not be more appropriate. In 1990 and 1991 the Jesuits are celebrating a double anniversary. On September 27, 1990 the Society of Jesus will celebrate the 450th anniversary of its approval as a religious order by Pope Paul III. In 1991 the 500th anniversary of the birth of St. Ignatius of Loyola will be celebrated. The two anniversaries will be combined into an Ignatian Centenary beginning on September 27, 1990 and finishing on July 31, 1991. We are deeply indebted to the Society of St. Paul for this most valuable contribution to the Ignatian Centenary.

Vincent O'Keefe, S.J.
Superior of Provincial House, Bronx, NY
Assistant General of the Society of Jesus
1965-1983

INTRODUCTION
WHO ARE THE JESUITS?

Six typical Jesuits

In San Salvador during the hours of curfew on the night of November 16, 1989, a detachment of soldiers burst into the residence of the Jesuits of the University of Central America (UCA) and killed six religious: Ignacio Ellacuria, Rector of the UCA, philosopher and theologian; Segundo Montes, sociologist and Director of the Institute for Human Rights; Ignacio Martín Baró, Vice-Rector and respected social psychologist; Amando Lopez, professor of theology and philosophy; Juan Ramòn Moreno, also a professor of theology and preacher of the Spiritual Exercises; Joaquin Lopez, organizer of radio schools of literacy for the Salvadorian peasantry.

The massacred community of the UCA mirrored in a little the whole Society of Jesus. It was a university community; and today, with eight thousand men involved in higher education and in universities, the Society is above all an Order of educators. It was a missionary community (five of the six murdered men had left their homeland, Spain, to labor in San Salvador); of the twenty-five thousand Jesuits, half are serving the Churches of Africa, Asia and Latin America. It was a community open to the needs of Salvadorian society, especially of the most marginalized part; throughout the world — from Chile to Lebanon, from

Madagascar to Sicily — the Jesuits are committed, for the Gospel's sake, to carrying on the struggle to liberate the poor and the oppressed.

Father Ignacio Ellacuria and his companions were typical Jesuits in another sense: for their severity towards themselves and the students of the UCA. They gave much and they demanded much. A serious attitude toward work is found among all Jesuits. But if you scratch a little beneath this quality, you will discover something else. You will discover lengthy preparation, self-discipline, the habit of weighing the means against the end. And if you scratch even further, you get nearer the roots and then need to talk of faith in Christ and of the will to communicate this to others, especially to those who humanly speaking are worst placed to receive it. And this was what their author and originator, Ignatius of Loyola, wanted the Jesuits to be.

The founder

Until he was thirty, Ignatius, scion of a Basque family belonging to the minor nobility, had pursued dreams of glory in the world of chivalry. He dreamed too of storming the heart of a great lady at court, with whom he was secretly in love. On May 20, 1521, at Pamplona, the whole direction of his life was changed by a cannon ball of the besieging French. Ignatius emerged from the engagement with a shattered leg. During his lengthy convalescence spent in the modest palace of Loyola, he asked in vain for books about chivalry. He was given *The Life of Christ* and *The Flowers of the Saints*. This reading matter worked his conversion; he concluded the life he had hitherto led to be folly and resolved on a radical change.

No sooner was he on his feet again than he left all and set off on pilgrimage to Jerusalem. He intended to take ship at Barcelona but unforeseen circumstances forced him to wait for more than a year. He spent this time at Manresa, where he had a number of fundamental mystical experiences, and where he preached and wrote the substance of the *Spiritual Exercises,* which were to form the basis of the future Society of Jesus.

Eventually he reached Jerusalem by way of Rome and Venice. He would have liked to stay in the Holy City for ever, but from certain signs he perceived that God wanted him elsewhere. He returned to Spain, studied grammar at Barcelona, then philosophy and theology for a year and a half at Alcalà. At the same time, he preached and gave spiritual direction. This layman who was going around usurping the functions of the priest aroused suspicions, and the Inquisition twice put him on trial. He was set free, but Ignatius realized he would benefit from a change of air.

In 1527 he went to Paris, where he met several students who shared his own apostolic zeal. In a chapel on the hill of Montmartre, he took a vow with six of them to live in poverty and go again to Jerusalem — with one proviso, that if, after a year spent waiting in Venice, the journey to Jerusalem proved impossible, the seven of them would put themselves at the disposal of the Pope, for him to employ on whatever apostolic tasks he pleased. This was in 1534.

In 1537 Ignatius was in Venice. For him and his companions, now increased to ten, the pilgrimage to the Holy Land was clearly out of the question. Waiting for the year to expire, most of them scattered into the university cities between Padua and Siena, while Ignatius and two of the others went to Rome. When they presented themselves to the Pope, he accepted them into his service. They then considered whether the right step would be to bring yet another religious Order into existence: of a new type, *contemplative in action.* They decided to do so. The new Order, called the *Society of Jesus,* was formally recognized by Pope Paul III in 1540. The following year, Ignatius settled near the little Church of the Madonna della Strada, where the Church of the Gesù rises today. There he wrote the *Constitutions* of the

Society, directed the activities of his missionaries, opened free day-schools in association with the colleges built to educate future Jesuits and maintained a voluminous correspondence with people all over the world. When he died, at dawn on July 31, 1556, the Society of Jesus already numbered more than two thousand members and its sphere of action comprised virtually all the countries of western Europe, Brazil, Ethiopia, India and Japan.

Persecuted and oppressed

During the next two centuries, the Society of Jesus experienced the most glittering successes and the most devastating persecutions. Missionary expansion continued unabated. The Jesuits (in the person of Matteo Ricci) reached China; they went to Spain's trans-Atlantic colonies and to North America. In Latin America, the Society created the *Reductions of Paraguay,* which in fact included Uruguay, part of Brazil and a vast area of Argentina. Freed from the servitude imposed on the local populations by the Spanish authorities and colonizers, the natives of these regions, under Jesuit guidance, organized a community life in which the economic, cultural and religious elements were harmoniously combined. A change of political wind in Europe was to signal the end of the *Reductions.*

In China and India, the Jesuits were ahead of their times in trying to adapt the historic forms of Christianity to the local cultures. They were not understood by the other religious missionary Orders, who denounced them to Rome. Rome first gave an evasive answer, then opted for tradition, that is to say, for the reassuringly familiar.

In the theological and spiritual sphere they aroused polemic too: Jesuits versus Dominicans on subtle questions concerning the relationship between divine grace and human freewill; Jesuits versus Jansenists on the way of interpreting and living the Christian life: tolerant and compassionate as regards the first, obsessively rigoristic as regards the second.

Outside Church circles, it did not help the Jesuits to be sought after by princes and kings as advisers and confessors. In court intrigues and dynastic disputes, willy-nilly the Reverend Fathers got caught up too. In a Europe split by the religio-political divide furthermore, these courageous, well-trained priests came to be regarded as dangerous enemies by the rulers of Protestant countries. An amalgam of diatribes, grudges, suspicions and conflicts inflamed an anti-Jesuit campaign which, beginning in the lifetime of Ignatius himself and full-blown by the middle of the seventeenth century, lasted for more than another hundred years. It produced a number of notable literary works (as for instance Blaise Pascal's *Provincial Letters*) and, more particularly, disgraceful libels in which the Jesuits were represented as the poisoners of kings, corrupters of the young and weavers of dark plots to achieve total power.

Caesaro-papism (the interference by secular rulers in ecclesiastical affairs), which characterized the policy of the European courts of the day, perceived the Jesuits to be its most powerful adversary: the Society's influence, exerted through its colleges, on the upper classes was much feared. Governments reacted by expelling the Society. The Jesuits were driven out of Portugal, dissolved in France, expelled from Spain and the American colonies. They were loaded into ships and dumped on the shores of the Papal States. Conditions on the voyage were particularly frightful. More than five hundred died.

On August 13, 1773, a heavier blow still! Yielding to the blackmail of a schism threatened by the Catholic sovereigns, Pope Clement XIV published the Brief *Dominus ac Redemptor* in which he suppressed the Society of Jesus. The Superior General of the day, Lorenzo Ricci, was imprisoned in Castel Sant'Angelo, where he suffered cold and hunger, and died two years later.

Rebirth

Thirty-seven years were to go by before another Pope, Pius VII, called the Society of Jesus back to life with the Bull *Sollicitudo omnium ecclesiarum* (August 7, 1814). Seven hundred ex-Jesuits instantly answered the summons, the majority of them coming from Russia where the Jesuits had retained their identity since the Empress Catherine II, being of the Orthodox faith, had refused to put the pontifical Brief into effect. In the first year of restoration, there were no fewer than seventy novices. By the end of the nineteenth century, the Jesuits numbered fifteen thousand. A time of stormy growth: despite the fact that new polemics, particularly ferocious with the Catholic liberals, resulted in the expulsion of the Society from the European states, its new foundations elsewhere put the expulsions in the shade.

Even during the twentieth century, the Society has been amassing expulsions: from Portugal, from Mexico, from Spain, and from Germany and Austria under Nazi rule. After the Second World War, the Jesuits were expelled from various communist countries. These measures seem to have actually strengthened the Order, which went on growing in membership and works. In 1965, the closing year of the Second Vatican Council, the Jesuits numbered thirty-six thousand.

The Council summoned by John XXIII affirmed the desires for renewal expressed by various sections of the Christian community; it developed their content and proposed them to the whole Church. The Jesuits made far from negligible contributions to this renewal of the Church, especially in the fields of biblical studies (scholars such as Fathers Stanislas Lyonnet, Xavier Léon-Dufour, Luis Alonso Sch

Decisive, even if more controversial, has been Father Pierre Teilhard de Chardin's contribution in rousing Christians to a more optimistic vision of the world (humanity and nature) and one inspired more by Christ's work of redemption.

The post-Conciliar tempest

In 1965, another Basque, Pedro Arrupe, was elected as twenty-seventh successor to the Basque Ignatius of Loyola. It fell to this slender and affable man, who had spent the greater part of his life in Japan (where he had witnessed the explosion of the atom bomb on Hiroshima), to guide the Society through the difficult post-Conciliar years. Difficult because the Jesuits, in common with most other religious institutes, were experiencing a sharp drop in numbers owing to defections and a scarcity of new recruits. Difficult, above all, because the renewal demanded also of the Society was not understood by all its members in a balanced way: there were those who, for fear of the new, thought only of applying the brakes; and those, too enthusiastic over novelties, who wanted to throw caution to the winds. Besides this, the entire Society was deeply concerned with the problems of misery and oppression endured by the peoples of the Third World. Many Jesuits, particularly those in Latin America, were pressing for the Order to abandon its old commitments and invest much more in promoting social justice. Arrupe shared this sense of priorities and under his government many initiatives for the promotion of human welfare came into existence and were rapidly developed, notably the Social Centers, true analytical and programmatic laboratories for changing the unjust structures of society.

Undoubtedly by the end of the 1960's, the Society of Jesus was giving signs of a certain uneasiness within the ranks. After lengthy preparation in all the outlying communities, Father Arrupe decided to convoke an Extraordinary General Congregation in 1974 to investigate the state of the Order and define how the ancient Ignatian rules should be applied in the modern world. Paul VI approved of this decision but recommended that the essence of the Society should not be a subject for discussion. Pope Montini followed the labors of the General Congregation most attentively and one day intervened to block a motion to extend the fourth vow (of special obedience to the Pope, still professed today only by the most highly trained Jesuits) to all members of the Order. Furthermore, maintaining that some of the General Congregation's decrees were too pressing, he asked to examine them himself before they were promulgated: as indeed was his right, since the Pope is supreme guarantor of the Society's Constitutions. Paul VI returned all the documents two months later; his comments "which had no bearing on their substance" became an integral part of the 32nd General Congregation.

Despite the freedom of debate occasioned by the General Congregation, despite also a batch of decrees to furnish clear demarcations, in Rome's view the Society or, to be more precise, a great many Jesuits still didn't seem to be marching in the right direction. Severe papal warnings came showering down: John Paul I, in a posthumous discourse, warned the Jesuits against "temptations to secularism"; John Paul II, the following year, made similar observations to the General Curia and the Provincial Superiors of the Society, urging "discipline" and "absolute loyalty to the magisterium of the Church and Roman Pontiff."

The Calvary of Father Arrupe

Father Arrupe was convinced the Society, taken all in all, was sound. He was however feeling the weight of his years and thought a new General might perhaps be able to make a better job of putting the Pontiffs' recommendations into practice. He therefore decided to set the machinery in motion for another General Congregation, at which he would present his own resignation. It would have been the first instance of this in the history of the Society, the Superiors General of which are elected for life; even so, the possibility had in fact been foreseen at the General Congregation which had elected Arrupe. John Paul II however took the view that a change of steersman would be premature, and asked Arrupe to postpone his resignation. When, in the summer of 1981, the General of the Jesuits was struck down by an illness that left him paralyzed, the Pope, in breach of the Order's Constitutions, named the elderly Father Paolo Dezza as his delegate with full powers over the Society. Dismay and some sharp criticism followed this unusual measure. After several months of tidying up, Father Dezza, with the Pontiff's consent, called the 33rd General Congregation of the Order. This convened on September 2, 1983, and lasted until October 25. The opening days were spent in very serious debate about the Society's situation. Voting to elect a new General took place on September 13. At the first ballot, and giving the lie to the most "informed" Jesuitologists, an outsider was elected: Peter-Hans Kolvenbach.

A linguist in command of the Society

Father Kolvenbach was born on November 30, 1928, at Druten, a small town about twenty kilometers from Nijmegen in Holland. His father was a bank official; his mother, Jacoba Johanna Petronella Domensino, was of Italian origin. Peter-Hans entered the Society of Jesus when he was twenty. Having completed his philosophy studies at Nijmegen, he was sent to Lebanon, where he took his doctorate in theology at the Université Saint-Joseph, Beirut. There, in 1961, he was ordained a priest in the Armenian rite of the Catholic Church. He next spent time studying oriental languages, specializing in Armenian language and literature. The choice of this particular field was not accidental: from his arrival in Lebanon, Kolvenbach had been a member of the Armenian rite Catholic Church. After further studies in Holland and France, the future General of the Jesuits completed his studies in the United States, where he specialized in spiritual theology.

From 1968 to 1974, Father Kolvenbach was professor of

general and Armenian linguistics at the Foreign Language Institute, Beirut. From 1974 to 1981, he was superior of the Jesuits of
the Vice-Province of the Middle East. Throughout these years,
the political crisis in Lebanon was growing worse, leading to
warfare between the various factions. Father Kolvenbach's study
was hit by shells on two occasions. From 1981 till the day of his
election as General of the Society, Kolvenbach was Rector of the
Pontifical Oriental Institute in Rome.

In the first, and hitherto only, press conference, given a
month after his election, the new General of the Society of Jesus
said, "My fellow Jesuits haven't told me the reasons for their
choice, and I prefer not to ask them. In the Society of Jesus, the
General, when elected, can neither accept nor decline: he merely
has to do his duty as General for the remainder of his life."

In his first letter to his brother Jesuits, he stated that he
didn't know the Society. To get to know it, he embarked on a
series of journeys throughout the world, he being used only to
going for long walks in Beirut and Rome. As a result, it proved
difficult to find convenient opportunities for the following interview, which eventually took place during the first half of July
1989, with a few adjournments into subsequent months. The
principal difficulty had however already been overcome, when, a
year earlier, Father Kolvenbach, having conquered his natural
reserve, consented to the idea of holding this extended conversation. I should like to thank him for having ultimately agreed "to put
himself in the hot seat."

Father Kolvenbach, over to you!

Peter H. Kolvenbach
MEN OF GOD: MEN FOR OTHERS

1

IGNATIUS' EXAMPLE

A "jubilee" for the Jesuits

We are on the eve of two anniversaries of importance to the whole Church and in particular to the Jesuits: 450 years since Pope Paul III's approbation of the Society of Jesus, and 500 years since the birth of your founder, Ignatius of Loyola. What preparations are you making for these two anniversaries?

Since they fall so close together, it seems sensible to me that we should hold a combined commemoration. We are going to celebrate a single centenary year from September 27, 1990, to July 31, 1991. I don't however think it would be appropriate to hold a triumphalist evocation of the past; I am also anxious to avoid any celebrations incurring expense. Our concern will rather be to improve on what we are already doing as a Society. I should prefer us to concentrate on Ignatian spirituality rather than on St. Ignatius' life, and to look more towards our future commitments than to the past achievements of the Society of Jesus.

Even so, we can't ignore the experience of your founder. Who was Ignatius of Loyola: an ascetic? a mystic? a gifted organizer?

Ignatius was certainly a mystic, even if not one like St. John of the Cross, for our founder's mysticism was that of apostolic activity. He was an ascetic, but not on the lines of St. Anthony of the Desert, for whom asceticism seems to have been the very purpose of life. Ignatius valued asceticism as a means for better responding to the apostolic vocation, in the sense that he began as an ascetic and then gradually changed, not for an easier life but to help souls, to use one of his favorite expressions. He was of course a gifted organizer as well, though he didn't like organizing for organizing's sake. The organized body that he created had a very precise purpose: to serve the Lord in the Church. But perhaps the most telling definition of Ignatius is the one he applied to himself in describing himself as a "pilgrim." He was this not only while trying to discover what his vocation was as he wandered about Europe and the Near East. He was a pilgrim even when sitting behind his writing-desk as General of the Society. He was ever seeking to discover the will of God, which explains why his mystical life was concentrated not so much on who God is but on what God wants. At the outset of his pilgrimage, Ignatius didn't consider founding a religious family, but the Lord led him to found one; he didn't have a congregation of priests in mind, but God led him to create one; he probably didn't consider founding colleges for the education of the young — no doubt because he loved to be on the move, whereas teaching forces one to stay in one spot — nonetheless the Lord asked him to found them. Ignatius of Loyola throughout his life retained the mystical attitude of a pilgrim, of one who seeks the will of God.

Ignatian discernment

Following this path, he needed signs to indicate what God's will was for him. How did he manage to identify these?

There is a phrase of Ignatius that Jesuits love to repeat: to seek God in everything. God can speak through every kind of circumstance. Certainly he speaks through the Church, and for Ignatius the voice of the Pope was virtually the expression of the divine will. God also speaks in history, in nature and in what Ignatius himself called the dialectic of desolation-consolation, which is in effect the purging of one's own desires in the crucible of the divine will. Ignatius was a man of desires, and whenever one desire became stronger than the others, he would ask himself whether this might correspond to what God planned.

But wasn't there a risk of confusing his own desires with God's will?

He countered this risk with discernment. In the life of the founder of the Society of Jesus there are very clear instances of this. After his conversion, Ignatius was convinced God wanted him to go to Jerusalem for some apostolic task. When the Church, through the Custodian of the Holy Land, pointed out to him that this wasn't the place for him, he was deeply disappointed but clearly saw that the Lord was calling him elsewhere. We see another example of discernment when, in Rome, Ignatius and his earliest companions were wondering whether they ought to go on living as a group of friends or become a religious family with rules and a superior. Only after discussion and prayer lasting several weeks did they become convinced that the Lord was asking them to become a body of religious, subject to a superior. In Ignatius' *Diary* we have a further interesting case of discernment. It was to do with poverty. The founder had to decide whether it was consistent with God's will that the Society should allow certain types of house to have incomes. In prayer, indeed in a sort of mystical struggle, he asked himself what the Lord really wished with regard to evangelical poverty and the use of material goods to apostolic ends.

What was the outcome of Ignatius' mystical struggle as regards poverty and the Society's work?

From this long and concentrated spiritual discernment, three types of work emerged: the professed house which has no income; colleges, which are based on a foundation; and churches, which may have incomes. Ignatius would have preferred everything to have been free but was forced to admit the impossibility of realizing so exalted an ideal. He was however determined that the Gospel spirit should permeate all, and hence would constantly repeat the words of Jesus: "Freely you have received, freely give."

How does this aspiration of making everything free manifest itself in the Society today?

By apostolic activity unsparing of self. This means two things: a willing acceptance of duties and commitments for which there is no corresponding economic return; and being prepared to give, by virtue of one's own personal dedication, far more than one could ever receive in recompense by way of pastoral or cultural results.

Ignatius as son of Rome

You have already mentioned that, in seeking to know God's will, Ignatius attached great importance to the Church. He lived at a time when the Church was undergoing grave crises, culminating in Luther's protest and schism. Your founder never adopted attitudes critical of the hierarchy of the Church?

Ignatius wasn't unaware of the human frailties and flaws in the Church of his day. Nothing, nonetheless, could separate him from the love that Christ manifests for his Church. Nothing could be further from Ignatius' spirit than an attitude of the type "Christ yes, Church no." And he didn't have a dream-Church, an ideal Church, in mind. On the contrary, he saw the Church as it really is, mysterious yet concrete, made up of characters some strong, some weak, of saints and sinners. He further expressed his loving devotion to the Church by his *Romanità,* by emphasizing that the mystery of the Incarnation of the Son, the Father's salvific work, continues under the Spirit within the visible Church of Peter. For Ignatius, at the heart of that divine-human reality which is the Church, is found the ministry of Peter — that Peter whom the Gospel shows us as a sinful man yet summoned to confirm his brothers in the faith, a weak one yet summoned to be the foundation stone of the Church. For the founder of the Society of Jesus, Rome is — for all the accidents of its history — the expression and privileged sign of the mystery of the Church Incarnate. Even so, in Ignatius, there is not the least tendency to papolatry. Veneration of the Pope yes, but without flattery or deviant conformism. By the same token, Ignatius didn't wish Jesuits to visit Cardinals too frequently, the latter in those days not being limpid examples of Christian living.

Your founder had charges brought against him by the Inquisition first in Spain and then in France. In Rome he was misunderstood by important churchmen like Cardinal Pietro Caraffa, who later became Pope. Didn't these personal experiences leave any trace?

It's true Ignatius did suffer at the hands of some churchmen and at those of the Inquisition. And possibly as a result of this, he became convinced, at the outset of the Counter-Reformation, that many of the ecclesiastical institutions of his day needed to be converted. Nonetheless, in his faith and in his love of Christ, he accepted the Church as the Word of God had ordained it to be. As background to the Ignatian rule of thinking with the Church there is the conviction that criticizing the Church in its visible aspect must — if the criticism is not made with love — inevitably involve throwing doubt on the mystery of the Incarnation, on the mystery of the Word dwelling among us by means of the Church. Convinced as he was that the Church is not an association intended by human beings but one instituted by God himself, Ignatius took an optimistic view of the Church. And this is why the Ignatian rules of orthodoxy, of thinking with the Church, begin with *alabanza*, with praise. Ignatius was certainly aware of the shortcomings of the Church of his day, but he understood how to transcend them. He was not a Savonarola for whom everything in the Church was dark, but neither was he so naive as to think that all was as it ought to be. He was convinced that Church reform was needed. And, what is more, he said that it was needed from head to foot.

One of the conversions of the Church Ignatius couldn't have foreseen is the one involving the rediscovery, consequent on Vatican II, of the nature of the Church as communion and its expression as such in community. In the example and spirituality bequeathed you by Ignatius, wouldn't you agree that, in contrast to this, a strong accentuation of the individual character of the spiritual journey predominates, with the religious community being regarded to some extent as fulfilling a supporting role?

It's true the fountain of Jesuit spirituality, I mean the *Spiritual Exercises* of Saint Ignatius, never mentions the community, seeming rather to prefer an individualized experience of the relationship between God and the world. There we read of being alone with God alone; this however isn't individualism but the call to personal responsibility on the journey away from sin and approaching grace. This assumption of personal responsibility is basically directed towards *koinonia*, to communion stimulating us to a lively relationship with God and with the world.

But do the Ignatian sources speak about community with reference to the Church and, in particular, the local Church?

The *Spiritual Exercises* don't speak directly about this. In the Society's *Constitutions,* the word community occurs four times but envisaging something other than the local community. Note furthermore that within the Society there exists a sort of tradition according to which any insistence on prayer in common clashes with our refusal to be transformed into a monastic congregation, and any invitation to a more intense community life gets rejected as an attempt to impose a conventual form of life, which doesn't accord with our particular charism. All this notwithstanding, the ecclesial reality of communion truly concerns the Society, and today various forms of prayer in common, of sharing and solidarity are on the increase. The *Spiritual Exercises* made together by a whole Province, the contribution made by all the Jesuits of a given region towards the drawing up of plans for the apostolate, towards the nomination of major superiors, towards the choosing of new undertakings: these are a few examples of the way we are growing in our concrete expression of communion. I might also add our growing collaboration, at all levels, with bishops, priests, religious and laity.

Present-day value of the Spiritual Exercises

You have just been mentioning the Spiritual Exercises. *What value do you consider this little Ignatian treatise has for today, given that many people think it's out of date in layout, not to speak of language?*

The little volume of the *Spiritual Exercises* is a work of the sixteenth century, with all that this implies as to language, world-view and theology. But there are two things about it that are special. As a work, it is truly open, as the semiologist Roland Barthes has pointed out. According to him, the *Spiritual Exercises* do not have a single author, but four: Ignatius himself, who however retires to make way for the person giving the *Spiritual Exercises,* to whoever is making them and, above all, to the Lord who acts within us. Furthermore, we are not dealing here with a book, like so many others, containing some doctrine or theologico-spiritual theory; it offers us a road to the Gospel, a road which Ignatius has already travelled and wants to show to others. The present-day value of the *Spiritual Exercises* is therefore bound up with personal experience of the Lord and a resolve to follow the Gospel, which mysteriously ever retains its living appeal.

In the Spiritual Exercises, *with all the techniques suggested by Saint Ignatius, isn't there the underlying claim that mystical results may be attained by force of will?*

I don't agree. What Ignatius is proposing is the mobilization of the entire human potential, so that each of us can realize in our day-to-day lives the vocation to which we have been called. For this reason the *Spiritual Exercises* aren't merely for religious or for monks and nuns. They're for everybody. Making full use of time, of nature and of every other means is not a will-directed technique to attain mystical results but rather corresponds with our duty to put ourselves before God in the everyday activities of our lives, to discover the presence of God, the creator and giver of every gift, and hence to live in the light of his love. Besides, everything develops in free style since Ignatius asks the guide to adapt the *Spiritual Exercises* to the person making them and to propose specific means and suggestions only if these are likely to bear fruit; otherwise it is better to omit them. The sole purpose is to know the Lord better and to walk with him.

In the Church, is the use of the Spiritual Exercises *on the increase or in decline?*

One particular form of the *Spiritual Exercises* has disappeared or is disappearing fast: doing them on the grand scale, with a hundred or more participants and a preacher dictating four meditations a day. Now, the *Spiritual Exercises* tend to be given on an individual basis, which is in fact a return to primitive practice since this was the method habitually followed by Saint Ignatius. Today too, another interesting method, also foreseen by our founder, is making headway: the *Spiritual Exercises* in everyday life for people who can't spend a week or a month in a retreat house.

Are there other aspects of Ignatian spirituality which strike you as being somewhat overlooked in the Society of Jesus today and which in your opinion ought to be salvaged?

First of all, let me make clear that Ignatian spirituality isn't the monopoly of the Society of Jesus. There are several other religious families and not a few lay movements that draw their inspiration from the spirituality of Saint Ignatius. As far as the Society is concerned, I may say we are constantly discovering insufficiently regarded aspects of Ignatian spirituality which need to be recovered. This happens with the *Spiritual Exercises*, which Jesuits make every year, and also with the annual colloquy every religious has with the major superior from whom he receives his mission. This rediscovery is due to the fact that Ignatian spirituality is a spirituality of tensions. The Society is simultaneously contemplative and active, universal yet part of a specific culture, organized as a community yet orientated towards mission. There is always a danger of losing the proper balance between these values in tension. Hence the need for a continual rediscovery of Ignatian spirituality. In recent years, two major features of the founder's charism have been re-emerging among us: discernment, and solidarity with the poor. Discernment is, as I have already pointed out, the search for God's will through prayer and the most extensive consultation. Solidarity with the poor, as Ignatius practiced it and asked his followers to practice it, today — having spent a long period of time somewhat in eclipse — is central to the Society's activities.

Apostles before all else

What Ignatius originally had in mind wasn't a religious Order consisting mainly of priests but a group of people properly trained as evangelists. If Ignatius were alive today, wouldn't he create, in addition to a religious institute, a lay movement no doubt of students and generous professional people along the lines of Communion and Liberation *or of* Opus Dei?

It's impossible to say. What however is certain is that, to Ignatius, this question would have sounded very odd. For him, what counted was to respond to the will of God. It's true he didn't have a religious institute in mind to start with, for the good reason that the religious of the day exhibited some degree of decadence. But once God had led him to grasp, by means of the Church, that he and his friends ought to become a body of religious, Ignatius hesitated no longer. It is equally true that in the early days after his conversion, the Society's founder thought neither of studying theology nor of becoming a priest. The apostolate was what interested him and prompted him to preach. But once he saw that to preach he would have to become a priest, and that to become a priest he would have to study, at the no longer tender age of thirty-five he began to study, attending the universities of Alcalà and Paris. In a word, what mattered to Ignatius was to be absolutely available to God's will. Works, apostolic strategies, pastoral plans would never have been absolutes for him.

Ignatius loved to present himself as a pilgrim, the follower of a poor and humble Jesus. In this respect he was also consistent in refusing all ecclesiastical dignities for his own followers. The past and present of the Society have taken other paths: is this, rightly seen, adapting to the times or it is a betrayal of his ideal?

No question but that in the sixteenth century ecclesiastical dignity was linked with political power and thus conferred a not inconsiderable social and economic advantage. So it was logical that Ignatius who preached and practiced evangelical poverty should not be ambitious for ecclesiastical dignities either for himself or for his followers. Another reason and possibly the main one, why Ignatius didn't want his followers to become bishops and cardinals had to do with the stability which these offices entailed. Ignatius founded a Society of missionaries ever ready to go anywhere in the world, having no fixed abode. It must be said however that when the Pope wanted to entrust a Jesuit with missions of peculiar difficulty, Ignatius certainly didn't try to evade this, even though they did entail episcopal ordination. Such was the case, for instance, with the first papal delegate to Ethiopia, who was one of Ignatius' companions. Today the Society still has a poor and humble Savior as its ideal and apostolic availability as its norm. The fact that now some Jesuits are bishops — ninety-three to be precise — doesn't conflict with that model and that norm, since today episcopal orders and the cardinalatial dignity are certainly not bound up with political power and economic advantage.

Ignatius intended and carried out an apostolic commitment principally among the humblest of the humble. After his death, the Society seems to have followed other paths: approaching and converting the mighty on the theory that their conversion would effect the conversion of their subjects, their inferiors. Here again: adapting to the times or betrayal of the ideal?

I can assure you, Ignatius was never exclusionistic or class-conscious but always harbored a truly catholic, that is to say, universal spirit. It was typical of his style, as well as of his deepest convictions, to try to approach everyone with apostolic intent. He certainly didn't disdain the mighty; a large correspondence survives between himself and kings, queens and nobles of every rank. It is equally true that he concerned himself with the poor, for their spiritual or social improvement. In this respect he was

very practical and wasn't ashamed to ask the rich to help the poor.
I might say he was a good follower of Jesus who was very free in
dealing with the social classes of his day: Christ preferred the
poor because of their greater availability to the Kingdom, but he
also accepted the invitations and friendship of those rich people
who showed signs of being open to God and who thus demonstrated their poverty of heart and non-attachment to earthly
things. Ignatius knew that Jesus died for all, for rich and poor, and
approached the one and the other with apostolic zeal. But Ignatius
was also a child of his times, in which the axiom *cuius regio, eius et
religio* held sway, obliging the subject to profess the religion of the
prince. In converting the mighty, Ignatius was able to observe the
domino effect right through society. It seems to me the Society
has always kept faith with Ignatius's example in not refusing
apostolic tasks for social reasons. It still persists along this road
today, similarly sharing in the preferential option for the poor, this
being a choice dictated by the Gospel, not by class interest: the
choice is dictated by love.

In his Letter to a Present-day Jesuit, *the theologian Karl
Rahner has Ignatius say that, at the outset, the Society was marginal to the Church and to society and that it should have no cause for
complaint if this were to be the case again today or in the future. Has
Rahner interpreted Ignatius right?*

It seems to me this reflection of Fr. Karl Rahner's can be
applied to all religious life, this not being an essential element in
the Church but a free gift of the Spirit. In this sense it may indeed
be said to be marginal to the Church but in the same sense, for
example, as prophecy, not being integrated in the Church, may
be considered marginal. In point of fact, the purpose of religious
life is to remind the Christian community of this or that aspect of
the Gospel message which, in the vicissitudes of history, may get
overlooked. When that happens, God raises up a Benedict of

Nursia, a Francis of Assisi or an Ignatius of Loyola and these once again set forth in the light those Gospel values in danger of being eclipsed. Furthermore, by our choosing to follow the Lord more closely by practicing the evangelical counsels, religious life reminds us that our fatherland is not in this world but in the Kingdom of God, the coming of which we await. Given the eschatological significance of religious life, it cannot be other than marginal to human society, since the latter, generally speaking, pursues quite different values.

2

JOYS AND SORROWS OF THE SOCIETY

Growing apostolic commitment

You have been the Superior General of the Jesuits for the last seven years. On being elected, you remarked that you didn't know the Society. After all your meetings with individuals and groups of Jesuits, and having received thousands of letters and made so many journeys, I imagine you now know your Order very well. How is the Society's pulse?

What I notice most of all is a rediscovery of Ignatian spirituality. A rediscovery which is initially orientated towards the *Spiritual Exercises* and then, gradually, towards the *Constitutions* and Ignatius' *Letters.* The Second Vatican Council, for its part, has encouraged the development of liturgical and biblical prayer in the Society: a new form of communal prayer is on the increase in our communities, culminating in concelebration of the Eucharist. Further, in the Society, union of hearts and minds, discernment in common, that is to say, the communal effort to discover the will of God, and the apostolic commitment to proclaim the faith and promote justice in the name of the Gospel are all on the increase.

What are the signs of the Society's growing apostolic commitment?

I think of the living witness of all those Jesuits, known, unknown or misunderstood, who live under regimes of open persecution or suffocating oppression, in peculiarly harsh material conditions, or in social environments where the Kingdom of God, far from approaching, seems ever further away. They live in obedience to the call to be a voice crying in a real wilderness. Beyond any grounds for hope, they obey their mission of hoping that the expectation of the rule of love, justice and peace will not remain a utopian dream. They live the paschal experience of seeing our best apostolic intentions uncomprehended, and of suffering, not only for love of the Lord's Church but also as a result of the tensions and divisions existing among the people of God. They are the signs of an apostolic zeal which would be inconceivable, were it not for that experience of God which can confer on our way of doing things the absolute stamp of faithfulness, of radical exigency and unconditional response — analogous to that of the Apostles — of which the Lord is pleased to have need for his Kingdom in the world.

There is however another side to the coin and, if I'm not mistaken, you have yourself on more than one occasion drawn attention to a certain discouragement, a sort of apostolic feebleness (atonia apostolica), *making the Society's task more difficult to discharge. What are the causes of these difficulties?*

The vocation of a soldier of Jesus entails the call, heard by Ignatius, to help souls. The response to this sort of call entails accepting the summons to be Jesus for others, his life and labors being marked by a clearly apostolic purpose. The moment however we try to adapt this project to our own day and age, a lack of daring may well induce us to doubt whether we shall be able to carry it out. Furthermore, the problems that expressions such as conversion, mission, defending the faith, spreading the Gospel, give rise to, thanks to their possible ambiguity, are not hard to imagine. But if, while striving to purge ourselves and embrace the inner dynamism of the Gospel, we give in to difficulties, we shall end up by admitting that the reason for belonging to the Society of Jesus has lost its incisive clarity. On the other hand we should empty our activity of that free collaboration which God is pleased to ask of us for the building of a more human and just world, were we to reduce the Society's apostolic dimension exclusively to the promotion of determinate causes, however just or of specific value, however good they might be. In our commitment, reference to the Gospel has to be explicit. For the Society to remain faithful to its apostolic vocation and its mission within and for the Church, it has to be constantly clarifying — by the light of the Spirit and through spiritual and apostolic discernment in common — its apostolic aims and options so that all its extraordinary human dynamism may remain plugged into the power of the Spirit continually at work in the world.

Perhaps I'm over-simplifying but it seems to me you're saying there's a weakening of the Society's missionary spirit. Now, the word mission means availability, openness to all, a characteristic that has distinguished the Society since its birth. Is it still so or are there now signs of a closing-in?

The Society's missionary link with the Apostolic See implies a vocation open to all the pressing cares of the Church. This makes us ready to go, especially by virtue of the fourth vow, to whatever part of the world apostolic obedience may summon us. The universal Church, for which the Holy Father has supreme responsibility, is always in need of help. The Society of Jesus, which the founder intended should be free of every territorial bond and of every particular service, can go to fulfil these needs at a sign from the Roman Pontiff, at whose disposal we have been put. This disposability continues to exist, even when forms of nationalism, provincialism and apostolic inertia manifest themselves. These are expressions of introversion and restrict our apostolic horizons to the solving of this or that conflict within the Church. They are, at the same time, signs of the refusal to situate every apostolic priority within a comprehensive vision, such as the universal Church has and the Society ought to have.

Ten thousand Jesuits fewer

I suppose some apostolic slowing-down may be due to the smaller number of men available now than the Society had in the past. Your Order has lost ten thousand members over the last twenty years. The crisis over vocations still continues, especially in Europe which even so is still the continent with the largest number of Jesuits. To what do you attribute the persistence of the crisis?

Perhaps the point ought to be made, to avoid any false conclusions, that the figure you've quoted doesn't cover just those Jesuits who have left the Society after committing themselves to it. It also includes those religious who have died and those who left the Order during their years of training. Even so, it's true that in Europe and other parts of what we call the First World the vocation crisis is still going on. The crisis is general, to some extent affecting all religious institutes and not merely the Society of Jesus. There seem to be many reasons for it. One explanation may be the falling birth-rate: in Christian families there are fewer sons and less generosity over allowing one of them to dedicate himself entirely to God. Another reason is perhaps the absence of spiritual vitality in our ecclesial communities. A third reason may be the diminishing attraction of austere apostolic labors that produce no immediate result. These reasons all play a role in the general situation in which the believing young find themselves today. It is no easy one. For the most part, they constitute a minority in their environment which, for a start, makes it harder for them to maintain their Christian identity. What is more, the world itself — in music and art, in sectarian and traditionalist movements, in various kinds of involvement in philanthropic activities — provides them with surrogate spiritualities in place of authentic Christian experiences. But there is yet another reason, and this in itself is a positive one, that is to say, the promotion of the apostolate of the laity, opening many opportunities for pastoral activity to the more sensitive and active Christian.

These are reasons possibly explaining the difficulty young men encounter over entering the Society. But isn't there also a problem over perseverance affecting those who have already entered?

Yes, there is; and this too isn't a problem unique to the Society of Jesus. Above all, in the First World today the young lack role-models of perseverance in family life, in the priesthood and also in religious institutes. The fragility of choices made, inconstancy: you may find these wherever you look. Besides, religious life calls for acts of renunciation. The renunciations are made for greater fullness of life; the sacrifice however is still there. Now, excessive insistence, even during the formation period, on self-fulfillment as the purpose of existence, risks making people overlook the fact that religious life is impossible without acceptance of the cross. Religious life is not something inhuman; it does however certainly run counter to the prevailing consumerism and freedom of self-expression of our day. To forget about this and talk merely about the positive qualities of our times doesn't assist perseverance in religious life one whit.

Does the decline in the number of Jesuits worry you very much?

Naturally this is a worry, especially since the apostolic demands and opportunities keep increasing while the apostles are growing fewer. This said, I should like to emphasize that we must avoid becoming obsessed by numbers. Religious life doesn't pull in the crowds. And what matters in serving the Church isn't the quantity but the quality. If we were to measure the importance of a religious family by its number of members we should indeed be on the wrong track.

Does the Society have a program for reversing the tendency towards a decline in membership and for obtaining a larger number of recruits?

Vocation is primarily a mystery of divine grace. And God encounters us as individuals by influencing our freedom of choice in the concrete conditions of history, with all the contingencies that this implies. True, the mission to which we are called obliges us to do everything within our power before humbly admitting that "we are unprofitable servants." It seems to me that promotion of vocations requires first and foremost that the whole Society should live its own vocation absolutely authentically. This means there is the requirement of renewal for every Jesuit and every community. More than ever before, in the surroundings and culture where they are growing up, the young people of today need to encounter people who can help them find Christ and discover the call that will fulfill their lives.

With what sort of tactics will this so-called strategic objective be pursued?

From meetings I've had with promoters of vocations in Western Europe, it emerges that it's no use thinking about promoting vocations unless on the basis of a more general activity in the world of the young. But we still need a specific service of discernment and personal preparation to offer those who feel themselves prompted towards religious or priestly life. The most effective means of reaching the young is still by personal contact. It is in personal relationship with the young that the appropriate word for arousing or revealing a vocation can be said. Hence there is need to mobilize the Jesuits once again to work among the young and develop the potential of relationships between the Society and the rising generations. We should exert ourselves to increase our capacity for listening and so be in a position to understand and recognize the expectations of the young. When appropriate, we should supply them with the words and explanations they need to describe and understand what is going on in the depths of their souls.

What can attract the young of today to the Society of Jesus?

Four aspects of the Society seem to me to be particularly suited to attracting the young to our way of committing ourselves to the service of the Gospel: a life in the Spirit, in which they too can share; the preferential love for the poor, for Christ's sake; the universality of our mission; a witness of a community life of friends in the Lord, even though ours aren't communities of monastic or conventual type. I might also point out that those who join us or intend to join us nearly always have a feeling for the apostolic mission. Hence the importance of the Society's missionary commitment. We ought, for our part, to be unambiguous in the way we serve the Church today and at the same time make bolder efforts to carry the Church into a world that doesn't know the Lord or knows him inadequately. We also need to give a witness of greater evangelical simplicity and express the thrust of the Ignatian charism in our spiritual life, in the seriousness of our self-surrender to God.

Crisis over lay brothers

Your Order is experiencing a critical shortage of vocations for lay brothers. Why is this?

This problem too is not confined to the Society of Jesus but affects the whole Church. The fact is that, since Vatican II, lay

brothers, of all religious, are those whose numbers have propor-
tionately dropped most sharply. Basically for three reasons: first
of all, the Church has such a tremendous need of priests that, in
concentrating on priestly vocations, the gift of the lay brothers'
vocation is easily overlooked. Secondly, what we have already
said about the promotion of the lay apostolate has had even more
effect here: many Christians who could be called to the religious
life as laymen probably don't take the decisive step because they
are already deeply committed within their own particular Christian community. Note this: I'm not saying that the lay apostolate
shouldn't be promoted. On the contrary, I see it as essential to
the Church. No, I'm merely interpreting facts. I do think however
that a great deal more might be done to foster every type of
vocation. The third reason for the vocational crisis over lay
brothers is a reflection of the crisis in religious life as such. This
crisis is possibly less manifest among religious who are also
priests, since these manage to conceal it within their priestly
commitments; lay brothers on the other hand have no alterna-
tives but this: either to live their religious life in totality or to give
it up.

*What is the present-day role of lay brothers in the Society? What
is their juridical position?*

Saint Ignatius wanted to reproduce all social life in its complexity within the Society. He recognized that social life com-
prises a diversity of gifts and vocations, and that this diversity
enriches it. So he wanted there to be lay brothers in the Society
as well. By giving them the title of coadjutors, he didn't intend to
make them persons at the service of the priests but collaborators
in the apostolic mission of the Society's priestly body. In this
sense, in our Order there is one unique mission, lived by each
according to his gifts.

If Ignatius wanted to reproduce the complexity of social life within the Society, why didn't he consider some sort of collaboration involving women?

He did consider collaboration of this sort in the early days of the Society; and indeed here in Rome several women did collaborate with Ignatius in his apostolic work. But pretty soon the founder saw that the spiritual direction of these ladies was taking up more of his time than the Society and its affairs all put together. From this and other factors, he deduced that it wasn't God's will for the Society to have a female branch. Ignatius further laid down that Jesuits were not, in institutional form at least, to undertake the spiritual guidance of female religious institutes, and this so as not to impede apostolic mobility. There are however a great many congregations of sisters which draw their inspiration from Ignatian spirituality, and a few which have adopted the *Constitutions* of the Society of Jesus. With these institutes the Jesuits have certain links over sharing work, but these never assume institutional forms.

Do you have a problem over reforming the juridical standing of the lay brothers?

A number of religious institutes, which we might term mixed, are coming round to the position of full equality between priests and lay brothers. As things are, the Holy See doesn't permit a lay brother to be the superior of a community containing priests. For us Jesuits, the question is a different one, since we are a priestly body and the brothers are collaborators. It is however a fact that, social and cultural developments of our times being what they are, the role of the lay brother is changing and many brothers are now assuming responsibilities that throughout the Society's history they never assumed before. And I should like to emphasize that the Society of Jesus wouldn't be what it is, were it not for the commitment and example of consecrated life given us by the lay brothers.

The contribution of the Third World

The Society's new recruits come mainly from countries in Asia, Latin America and Africa. What effects will this produce on the now predominantly Western physiognomy of the Society?

Here again we find ourselves faced with a phenomenon affecting the whole Church: vocations to the priestly and religious life are on the increase in the Third World and on the decline in the West. It's only to be expected that the Churches of the Third World should now repay the apostolic support they received in times past, above all during the last century, from the Churches of the First World. Insofar as the Society is concerned, being an international Order, it has always experienced these waves of vocations, which have conferred specific cultural tints in successive periods. To begin with, there was the predominance of Spanish Jesuits, then of Italians, next there was a wave of Frenchmen, then we had the period of the Slavs, more recently that of the Americans. Now there is a significant increase in vocations in India. All this contributes to the richness of the Society's spiritual and cultural life. At the same time, the priorities of our more numerous Provinces inevitably permeate the apostolic consciousness of the entire Society. As in past years, under the Latin American influx, the Jesuits became more sensitized to the option for the poor, so today and in the immediate future no doubt we shall grow ever more sensitive to the apostolic problem of how to inculturate the faith in India and in Asia in general.

In which countries and in what environments does your apostolate encounter its greatest difficulties?

Every cultural area presents great difficulties. In what we call the First World, the West, we are trying our hardest to find the most suitable methods of re-evangelizing a society in which religious indifference is very widespread. The Society is aware of the need for true apostolic zeal in this environment, but the steps to be taken are far from easy. Making the task more difficult is the fact that the decrease in vocations is found above all in the First World. In the Second World, the main difficulty used to be the lack of religious freedom; today how ever in many socialist countries, and in the Soviet Union in particular, great changes are taking place. In the Third World, the problems are no less difficult. In Latin America, the great difficulty is how to translate the preferential love for the poor into concrete terms in countries where those responsible for monstrous acts of injustice and oppression, themselves claim to be Catholics. In Asia, the most difficult task is to find ways of helping the young Christian communities to bear witness to the Gospel in a world which numerically, culturally and religiously speaking is completely alien to the Church.

And where do you get the greatest apostolic satisfaction?

Wherever the Church is growing, thanks in part to the competent and generous-hearted help of the Society, and when this is recognized by the Pope and bishops. There is also great satisfaction in knowing how apostolic collaboration is developing between the various categories in the Church. I ought to mention in connection with this that many of the Society's works couldn't be carried on without the help of the laity. This is an important aspect of growing and effective communion within the Church. Among all Christians — bishops, priests and laity — awareness of being God's people, together proclaiming and preparing the Kingdom of God, is on the increase.

Jesuit martyrs

Not a few Jesuits have been killed over the past decades for reasons connected with apostolic commitment. In which areas have most Jesuits been martyred?

In the last fifteen years alone, thirty-two Jesuits have been killed because of their ecclesiastical or humanitarian activities. They cannot all be called martyrs in the technical sense of the word, since not all of them were killed out of hatred for the faith. In Latin America, the continent where we have seen the highest number of our brothers killed, their commitment to and with the poor has the effect of provoking to violence those people who do not want to change unjust social structures. This was also true in the case of the six Jesuits of the University of Central America in San Salvador.

Did you know Father Ellacuria and the five other murdered Fathers?

I met them a year before they were killed. They escorted me to the place where Archbishop Oscar Romero and, before him, another Jesuit, Fr. Rutilio Grande had been murdered. I could tell they were aware that the Lord might ask their lives of them as participation in his Passion and that they had already made the gift of them. By their sacrifice they have shared the fate of hundreds of other men and women, victims of battle and reprisal, subjected to the hellish round of violence and death.

In what other regions has the society lost members owing to violence?

A number of Jesuits have been killed in Africa, also because of their commitment in favor of the poor. In Lebanon, a number of our brothers have lost their lives while trying to help people stricken by the bombardments. In China, several Jesuits have died in prison because of their loyalty to the universal Church.

In the Society, what causes most joy and what occasions most grief?

Let me begin with the grief. The worst is that of not being able to perform all the work the Church counts on us to do, whether because we don't have the ability to do it or because our weakness prevents us from succeeding. Today, for instance, there is the urgent problem of training aspirants to the priesthood in Africa. There are many young men in the seminaries but a scarcity of teachers. The Society is constantly being asked to help in this area, and recently we agreed to take over the running of a seminary and to collaborate in a university, but we are well aware that our input falls short of what is needed. Similarly it is a grief to realize we haven't trained the men necessary for the tasks the Church is constantly taking on: dialogue with the major religions, for instance. Lastly, we grieve when a Jesuit leaves the Society for reasons which do not seem to coincide with God's will.

But there are joys too, aren't there?

Yes, there are. It is a joy to know the Society is working hard and well all over the world and making efforts constantly to do better. In all the Jesuits, I see a great availability to abandon this or that work to consecrate themselves instead to whatever activities may seem more urgent to the Church. There is missionary zeal within the Society, a promptness in responding to the appeals of local Churches that ask for our help. I had proof of this, for instance, when I recently asked for some Jesuits for Cuba: those ready to go far outnumbered the few I wanted.

3

THE POPE AND THE JESUITS

Back to normality

You were elected Superior General of the Society of Jesus on September 13, 1983, in the course of the 33rd General Congregation of the Order. This General Congregation marked the end of a difficult period which had culminated in John Paul II's entrusting Father Paolo Dezza with the extraordinary government of the Society. How have the Jesuits reacted to the Society's return to juridical normality?

In 1984 I asked the Superiors and Consulters of the Provinces to inform me about the reactions of the Society to the 33rd General Congregation. In response I received more than one thousand five hundred letters, that is to say, seventy percent of what I had asked for. On the basis of this mass of answers, much oral evidence and many meetings of every sort, I am in a position to declare that the first result of the General Congregation, that is to say, the return to normal government, thanks to the fundamental unity of the delegates (which some people deemed problematic, if not impossible) has been received favorably by the whole Society. This result put an end to a period of doubts and anxieties; it restored faith in the Society as an apostolic body, constantly able to rediscover its Ignatian charism and respond to the appeals of the Holy See and of our times; capable too of absorbing in all its vastness the spiritual heritage of the most recent General Congregations and of Father Pedro Arrupe. The return to normal government was accompanied by unanimous gratitude to Father Paolo Dezza and his assistant, Father Joseph Pittau, for the clear-sightedness with which they had discharged their difficult and delicate task. It was then too, I should like to mention, that Father Arrupe's official resignation as General of the Society was received, and the General Congregation paid him the tribute of its deep gratitude. I am sure that the best way for us to express our indebtedness to Father Arrupe is to put the 33rd General Congregation's exhortation into practice: "Today, rather than new and lengthy declarations or new decrees, we ought to put into effect that which has been handed down to us, for love should manifest itself in deeds rather than words."

Today all is serene between the Society of Jesus and the Holy See. Is this the result of a change of heart on the Society's part or of a diplomatic stance, of prudent tactics?

On this score, the Society had no need for any radical change of heart, since our spiritual outlook is clear, even if its embodiment requires growth, research and ongoing effort. From Saint Ignatius to Father Arrupe, the Society has always regarded its loyalty to the Vicar of Christ as a principle constituting the very reason for its existence. Father Arrupe had clearly stated as much in his last report on the *State of the Society,* in which he wrote: "Loyalty to the Vicar of Christ and the hierarchy of the Church is so fundamental an element of the Ignatian charism that guaranteeing it in all its fullness constitutes the very essence of the Society." Which is no more than putting into modern terms those words of Ignatius already in the *Formula* of the Institute and subsequently repeated word for word in the *Constitutions:* "All who make the profession in this Society should understand at the time, and furthermore keep in mind as long as they live, that this entire Society and the individual members who make their profession in it are campaigning for God under faithful obedience to our Holy Lord the Pope and his successors in the Roman pontificate."

"The Jesuits" — a novel

The book The Jesuits *by the ex Jesuit Malachi Martin caused a certain amount of fuss when published a few years ago. According to the author, John Paul II was on the point of suppressing the Society. What is your view?*

I've read the book and Malachi Martin's earlier novels (about the last Council and about the Vatican). I think he has a novelist's fertile imagination and that his book *The Jesuits* is first and foremost a novel from which the obligatory disclaimer has been omitted: "Any resemblance to actual people or events is purely accidental." Martin has not only overlooked this disclaimer but goes on maintaining that he has written the truth. Well, that's a fine claim for someone who makes so many mistakes, even elementary ones, about the Society and about Rome in spite of having spent so many years in the Society and in Rome. I repeat: as long as you take the book as a novel, it has a certain interest; if however you want to find the true facts of the case, then it is very misleading indeed. Martin represents me, for example, as talking to people whom I have never met in my life.

The nub of Martin's book is the intention of John Paul II and some of the Cardinals to dissolve the Society, since they perceived it as hostile to the Pope's pastoral policy. What is your view?

It's completely unrealistic to imagine that the Society can set itself up against the Pope. History and the present-day life of the Jesuits alike demonstrate that we are always ready to take on the missions that Pontiffs entrust to us. To dissolve the Society would therefore be no less than a self-inflicted wound; it would amount to destroying a significant apostolic work within the

Church. Admittedly the Pope may want to change a General or some other major superior and it is within his powers to do so, but it is completely unrealistic to think that he intends, or in the past intended, to abolish an Order which is laboring as hard as it can to serve the universal Church and the local Churches.

All the same, there has been a precedent, little more than two hundred years ago, when Pope Clement XIV suppressed the Society.

That was a different story altogether! Then the Pope was under pressure from various European governments. It was a political question or, more precisely, political blackmail, since Spain, Portugal and France demanded the suppression of the Order as a condition for restoring religious peace to the Church. Today, thank God, the Church is no longer so vulnerable, politically speaking.

The fourth vow is not discriminatory

The Jesuits' obedience to the Pope is expressed, in a certain number of cases, by the fourth vow, pledging special availability to the Pontiff. How did the idea of this individual link with the Pope come about?

Again I must quote the *Constitutions*: "Those who first united to form the Society were from different provinces and realms and did not know into which regions they were to go, whether among the faithful or unbelievers; and therefore, to avoid erring in the path of the Lord, they made this promise or vow in order that His Holiness might distribute them for the greater glory of God. They did this in conformity with their intention to travel throughout the world." Living this formula existentially, the first companions knew and felt themselves to be churchmen, personally and communally responsible, like the

Apostles united round Peter, for serving a hierarchically organized Church.

These reasons obtained more than four hundred years ago; do they still hold good today?

Greater efforts have been made to define and evaluate the exact scope of this special ecclesial link of the Society. Many attempts have been made to translate it into the various theological and cultural languages of our own times. Notably these have helped us understand more about the practical quality of Ignatius' mysticism. Be that as it may, no amount of effort has succeeded in throwing any doubt on either the existence or the exigency of this characteristic for us Jesuits of the twentieth century. To avoid all misunderstanding and prevent any possible abuse, the bounds delimiting the scope of the fourth vow would need to be traced with all due juridical precision. Nonetheless, it is still obvious that the important thing is not the canonical delimitation as such, but the Ignatian idea of our being in the Church. This idea has the power to inspire us to take a clear-cut yet onerous spiritual decision. By entering the Society and pronouncing the vows in accordance with the *Constitutions*, the Jesuit of his own freewill assumes a vocation and a precise mission within the Church; he cannot therefore renounce the ecclesial character of this vocation and of this mission, handed down from Saint Ignatius. And so today too, there are brothers of ours who, for the sake of this fidelity, are obliged to spend their lives in a hostile environment, deprived of religious freedom, even of freedom pure and simple. Faithful to the mission entrusted to us by John Paul II on the eve of the 33rd General Congregation, to proclaim the faith and promote human rights, the vast majority of Jesuits — in a multiplicity of apostolic tasks — embody and exemplify that devotion to the Church which is the hallmark of the Society.

Isn't the fourth vow a form of discrimination against those Jesuits who don't take it?

Ignatius had a deep respect for the diversity of gifts, of vocations and of ministries. For him, having a different vocation didn't instantly mean being the object of discrimination, as is too easily thought today. For Ignatius, the diversity of charisms constituted riches for the Church, contributing to its universality. While in Rome, he knew Philip Neri, for whom he had a high regard, but he never thought him less of an apostle for having confined his ministry to Rome and not departed, like Francis Xavier, for India and Japan. Similarly, within the Society, Ignatius knew there were Jesuits called to be itinerant apostles and Jesuits called to a more residential work; there were those drawn to serve the Lord in the intellectual field and those inclined to serve him with manual labor. For Ignatius, the diversity of gifts corresponded to a diversity of ministries. By the same token therefore there were Jesuits capable of responding to the special missions of the Holy See, to which they bound themselves by the fourth vow, and there were those who did not have this immediate and explicit vocation. All know that the Society of Jesus as such is called to respond to the tasks the Pope entrusts to it, and that all Jesuits have their share in carrying out such tasks. But this is brought about by means of the diversity of gifts God has given to each of us. People today find this organic conception of the Church hard to grasp, and as a consequence any diversity is judged to be discriminatory and only the equality of ministries appears to guarantee justice. But the categories of the Kingdom of God follow a logic of their own.

The problem of the fourth vow was however raised at the Society's last two General Congregations and, if I'm not mistaken, the majority of delegates at your 32nd General Congregation asked for the fourth vow to be extended to all Jesuits. The intervention of

*the Holy See alone blocked this request. Does this mean that the
greater part of the Jesuits have lost what you call "Ignatian
inspiration"?*

Even we Jesuits are subject to the influence of history and
the tendencies of human society. This explains how, in applying
the vision of Saint Ignatius, even the Society can err. I do
however believe that our 32nd General Congregation had no
intention of abolishing Saint Ignatius's ordinance, but rather intended to change its practical application, which in certain respects no longer corresponded with what Ignatius had wished.
The difficulty arose from the fact that an attempt was made to
abolish what was out of date without having positive propositions
to put forward about how Ignatian inspiration should be lived
today.

And that was when the Holy See intervened?

Yes, but this should come as no surprise, since in accordance with our *Constitutions* the Holy See has the responsibility of
seeing that we remain faithful to the Society's original charism. I
can give you an example of how this vigilance has been exercised
in another sector, giving rise however to a different outcome. We
have altered our rules about religious poverty, because the social
and economic changes of our times require a different style of
poverty from that practiced in the times of Ignatius. It was a
matter of being faithful to the Ignatian inspiration, yet expressing
it in the idiom of our own epoch. In this case the Holy See raised
no difficulties, since we had submitted very clear proposals from
which it was evident that it wasn't our intention to abolish the old
rules about poverty, but rather to live poverty according to the
spirit of those rules today. Perhaps we didn't have the foresight to
do the same thing over the fourth vow.

*The 32nd General Congregation wasn't proposing to abolish
the fourth vow but actually to extend it to every Jesuit.*

The proposal of that General Congregation was inspired by a Conciliar text, according to which, within one religious family, distinctions were not to be drawn except in relation to the Sacraments (in practice, the distinction between priests and laity). Now, it is indeed true that what was being proposed wasn't the abolition but rather the extension of the fourth vow to all Jesuits; equally however it was forgotten that the fourth vow is linked to the priesthood, since the apostolic missions entrusted to the Society presuppose priestly ordination. Be it said though that not all Jesuit priests pronounce the fourth vow, since this requires them to have the best dispositions for discharging a special mission entrusted to them by the Pope. That is to say, an individual training is needed and certain special gifts, among which priestly ordination. By the fourth vow, Saint Ignatius intended to offer the Pope excellent men for a greater service. Difficult phraseology for an age like ours, in which equality is sought and the word discrimination springs easily to the lips. But I want to emphasize that here we are concerned with service, not with power or the wielding of influence. So it seems to me that the Pope, to whom this duty of service is due, was within his rights to ask that the conditions governing that service should not be abolished. To extend the fourth vow to all Jesuits without distinction would in effect be to weaken the conditions for that greater service.

How has the Society reacted to the Holy See's request that the extension of the fourth vow to all Jesuits should not be discussed?

We have grown more mature, for the request has helped us to a better understanding of how we should give the Church a specific service which accords with the charism and intentions of our founder.

Does the proposal to extend the fourth vow to all Jesuits no longer exist, or has it gone underground?

Only those unfamiliar with Ignatian spirituality or the Society's commitment to the Church can suppose that it persists underground.

What are the conditions for a Jesuit to be admitted to the fourth vow?

The conditions have to do with the vigor with which he lives his religious life, his intellectual abilities as demonstrated by success in studies, the good showing given in this or that ministry. This last condition is a change from the past, when it was customary to take almost exclusive account of success in theological studies; today, excellence is assessed as it was in early days, account also being taken of qualities displayed in preaching, pastoral activity and government.

Who assesses this excellence?

The first assessment is made by a few Jesuits who are deputed for the purpose. Their recommendation is then examined by the Provincial Superior with his Council. Finally, there are the deliberations of the Superior General who, having taken the advice of his counsellors, summons the candidate to make solemn religious profession of the four vows.

Out of some twenty-five thousand Jesuits, how many have been called to pronounce the additional fourth vow of special obedience to the Pope?

This of course only applies to priests; there are 17,502 of them in the Society. In 1989, there were 1,953 Jesuits in simple vows; there were 5,630 who had taken solemn vows; and 9,919 who had taken all four vows, that is to say, 63.8%, which shows a slight increase over the previous two years (63.1% in 1988, and 62.5% in 1987).

The Church is not a parliament

I should like to ask you about some topics of the day, in connection with the Society's special relationship with the Pope and more with the Magisterium of the Church. In the spring of 1989 you ordered Jesuits not to make public statements on controversial topics unless they had first discussed them with their superiors. By acting like this, aren't you treating people who are in fact famous authorities in the sector in which they might wish to intervene (in theology for instance) as though they were under age?

I was merely reminding Jesuits of a rule we have had for a long time; also that no member of the Society should forget when making public statements on pastoral matters that he is to some degree involving the whole Order. It's a matter of perspective; some don't perhaps see this as clearly as others. Now, of course, if you think of the Church as a parliament in which all may and should speak, since truth is the product of debate, then to be able to make or not make a statement raises the problem: restriction or suppression of freedom of speech. But this is not the right way of looking at the Church, the people of God. The Lord Jesus is in the Church and he has revealed the truth about God and the truth about humankind. This is a truth that has been given and which no one can discard to suit himself. I recollect the Pope himself once saying at a meeting, "They can't expect me to alter the Gospel." I am very fond of the imagery of the Fathers, according to which the Church is like the mystery of the light; for us in the darkness of earth the light of the moon is not what lights us but the light of the sun which the moon is merely reflecting, so the truth that comes to us from the Lord is guarded and transmitted by the Church. And in the Church, the task of watching over the truth, of telling us what that truth is that the Lord has revealed, pertains to the Pope and his fellow bishops: not to the theologians, even though the latter are also serving divine truth.

I believe most theologians would have no objection to what you are saying, except to observe that even the Magisterium is obliged to use a terminology and hence a theology when transmitting the truths of the faith. And indeed the problem now in debate is that of the relationship between faith and theology.

True, and precisely with regard to this relationship it must be stated that the respective tasks of the bishops and theologians are not on the same footing. The clearest example of how this relationship ought to be, comes to us from Vatican II. Yes, it was certainly due to the theologians that the Council was able to present the Church with such fine texts, but the people who voted on these documents, the ones who decided whether they conformed to the faith of the Church, were not the theologians but the bishops, many of whom may well have been less competent theologically than the theologians who had been working in the background as experts.

To return to your question, it seems to me that, when making public statements on religious topics, we should always keep certain factors in mind: on the one hand, we must be aware that the truth has been given to us; on the other, faith and theology are not absolutely interchangeable, since they belong on different levels. I'm sure this is all perfectly clear to theologians, but the people of God at large run the risk of not understanding these distinctions and may thus be led to confuse the opinions of theologians with the truths of the faith. Add to this the simplifications or the condensations with which nine times out of ten the mass media treat these matters, and you'll have to admit the confusion caused can be both great and grave.

So the theologians ought to keep quiet even when the Magisterium adopts debatable positions?

It's not my business whether they keep quiet or not. Their freedom of research is assured, but they ought to behave responsibly when it comes to publishing the results. In these times of evident moral confusion, when the people of God no longer have the religious training that possibly they received in the past, we risk encouraging doubts and indifference. Saint Ignatius avoided criticizing the authority of the Church, even when perhaps he had more than one reason for doing so, so as not to diminish that authority as such. I think his example is still valid today. In other words, theologians ought to realize that they have a pastoral responsibility in their dealings with the people of God, and bear in mind that not everything they say or write for love of the Church actually builds up the Church.

Are you saying that, within the Church, criticism should be outlawed?

No, I believe even criticism can help the Church. But it must be criticism explicitly inspired by faith and by love for the Church. Systematically negative, aggressive and polemical criticism cannot build up the Church.

Limited calls to order

Have you had to take measures against Jesuits in Germany, France, Spain and Italy, who, with other Christians, have signed documents levelling criticism against the hierarchy of the Church?

No, I merely published the reminder which we have just been talking about. Those Jesuits who, since then, have signed documents of the sort you mentioned, did so with the consent of their local Superiors. To deal with this problem, we in the Society are making a drive to collaborate with Bishops' Conferences and so air the difficulties that theologians may encounter in certain fields; without, that is, having recourse to the simplifications and pressures of the press. I think a procedure of this sort would help towards solving the problems of which we've been speaking. By the same token, I'm convinced that within the Church there ought to be mechanisms or organs by means of which problems can be sorted out when these occur. And I also think that Bishops' Conferences ought to start setting up committees of bishops and theologians to deal with difficult situations and problems. It is good for the people of God to know that this is being done and that difficulties will be dealt with in love of truth, to the benefit of the whole Church.

Since you became Superior General of the Society, how many Jesuits, whether theologians or not, have you had to reprimand?

Ten at the most.

What forms have your reprimands taken?

In the case of theologians, I simply had to ask them not to teach theology any more. So far, there have only been three cases of these: one in India and two in Spain, at Granada. All three of these brothers accepted my ruling. Other episodes were solved autonomously within the confines of the theological faculties concerned, by discussion and deeper consideration of theses certainly very bold but with little basis.

Did you intervene on your own accord, or were you asked to do so by the Holy See?

Not so much by the Holy See as by the Bishops' Conferences. The three Jesuits in question were helping to train local clergy in the seminaries and theological faculties. Since the bishops are ultimately responsible for training the clergy, I thought it was perfectly in order for them to turn to the Superior General of the Society and ask for measures to be taken against Jesuits whose teaching, in the bishops' judgment, wasn't in conformity with the Magisterium of the Church.

What points of Church doctrine were at issue?

In the case occurring in India, the issue was ecumenism: the Jesuit concerned was exaggerating ecumenical openness to such a degree that Christianity was being watered down. As regards the two theologians of Granada, they had aligned themselves with the so-called People's Church, which rejects the hierarchical structure of the Church universal.

That sounds more like a Latin American problem. Haven't you ever had to reprimand Jesuit theologians working in Latin America?

For the substance of their teaching — never. I am at present examining the case of a Latin American Jesuit theologian, whose merit isn't in question but whose method of teaching is, since he is excessively critical, I might say aggressive, in his treatment of the institutional Church. He too helps in the training of future priests and one may well wonder in what state of mind seminarians, who have heard continual criticism of the Church to which they intend to pledge their entire lives, can advance to priestly ordination.

To live the Council requires a change of heart

In your opinion, are the expressions of protest, such as the publications of the theologians whom we've already mentioned, due to a spirit of rebellion, or are they a sign that, within the Catholic Church, the room for dialogue opened up by Vatican II is now becoming more and more restricted?

From Ignatius, I've learned to take a positive view of whatever goes on in the Church. Since the Second Vatican Council, which reminded us that the Church is communion, the various components of the people of God have been seeking their individual vocations, their individual missions. Indeed the whole Church has taken the road to respond more effectively to the command to evangelize, and on this road each of us has a specific contribution to make. We are however only human and, as we search out what our contribution should be, crises, tensions and problems may well arise. I see all this ebullience as the outward face of an intensely lively organism, striving for equilibrium in all sorts of fields: in relations between bishops and theologians, in the relationships between local Churches and religious Orders, in collaboration between the various forms of lay apostolate. The dialectic between criticism from theologians or from other ecclesial entities and the complaints of the hierarchy also forms a part of this process of growth towards ever greater communion. Clearly, if in the criticism violent, aggressive expressions are used, an equally violent response can be expected. In the Church, the law of charity ought to regulate all our behavior, even our protests, but it is hard to die to oneself and so there will always be instances of resistance dictated by a worldly spirit. This notwithstanding, I'm convinced we're growing in communion and that the spirit of dialogue reintroduced into the Church by Vatican II will continue to bear fruit. It is a spirit that can't be stifled for the good reason that Pope John Paul II is its constant guarantor.

On the subject of Vatican II, do you consider that the Council has been presented in a one-sided interpretation, particularly by progressive Christians?

I think we ought to go beyond these labels of progressive and conservative. Labels like these are handy but often they oversimplify. Vatican II was a gift of the Holy Spirit to the Church in order to make it more able to discharge its mission in the modern world. It would be wrong therefore to think of Vatican II as a disruptive event in the Church's life. As it says in the Gospel, in the Church's treasury there is new and old: *nova et vetera*. It seems to me that, in certain sectors of the Church, people don't always bear this continuity in mind and adopt an attitude of breaking with the past. By so doing, they run the risk of forgetting that the Church is forever the same, the Church of the Apostles. It's a Church conserving the deposit of faith and, at the same time, it progresses in its understanding of the mystery of Christ and in its spreading of his message. Like all living organisms, the Church proceeds by development, not by rupture.

How should one assess so overt a rebellion against Vatican II as that of Archbishop Lefebvre and his followers?

It's a very sad episode in the Church's life, even though it's common knowledge that the opposition to Vatican II which he has made visible had been brewing for ages in sectors of the Catholic world in reaction to the mistaken way in which some of the reforms intended by Vatican II have been applied. I'm thinking in particular of the wild experiments carried out in the liturgical field, despite directives to the contrary from the Holy See and the Council itself. I don't intend to justify the conduct of Archbishop Lefebvre and his followers however, for they have broken communion with the Church, having confused Apostolic Tradition with the traditions and customs of their own religious upbringing. A Council is always a gift of God, but to receive it properly we need to have a change of heart. To live a Council requires a conversion. So it's not to be wondered at if there has been and still is resistance to Vatican II. This will go on until we have purged our hearts, to make them gladly willing to accept the great obligations that the Council demands.

In your view, was Vatican II a purely pastoral Council?

In this Council, the doctrinal affirmations can't be separated from the pastoral guidelines. Similarly in the Church at large, pastoral activity can never be divorced from doctrine, since every apostolic commitment is inspired by the Gospel message, by the vision of God and humankind revealed to us by Christ. One might, I suppose, say Vatican II wasn't a doctrinal Council in the sense of those Councils summoned in the past to put an end to great theological controversies and to combat certain heresies. But it was highly doctrinal in two other senses: it completed a vast review of the Christian message in order to make it easier for people to understand today, and it published several great dogmatic Constitutions, like the ones on the Church and on divine revelation.

The tensions in the Church don't seem to deal only with the relationship between theologians and Magisterium. There are tensions too in pastoral practice, in the method of organizing and living Church life, and these are acute enough for there to be talk of different Church models. How does the Society stand on this?

Here again Saint Ignatius' example is valuable. He knew from personal experience — and the Rules confirm this — that the breath of the Spirit, going in search of a body in which to realize the incarnation of God-with-us is the bringer of fire and tempest, tension and conflict. Ignatius lived out this tension to the full between a personal religious experience (to which he responded with his whole personality) and service to the historic and social body of the Church. Even if he had no knowledge, as we have, of the possible tensions between different Church models, he experienced some of their consequences. I'm talking of tensions, not about contradictions. One same loving gesture of the Father, in communion with the same Spirit, indissolubly unites Christ and the Church in the relationship of bridegroom and bride. And hence it is not possible to divide what the Lord has united in the mystery of Christ and his Church. Our own behavior ought to follow from this. We ought to suffer over the divisions and conflicts, and refuse to do anything whatever to contribute to them. We ought to take an active share in initiatives to promote a fuller unity. And we ought to ask constantly that the prayer of

Jesus may be fulfilled: "That they may all be one, as we are one."
If this were so, different Church models would never so much as
be suggested, were any antithesis between base and hierarchy
intended in them; they would on the other hand be legitimate if
conceived to meet the need to embody the Christian message in
different historic and social situations.

Communication between the Holy See and the Society

*Again you insist on the unity of the Church. Now, it's obvious
that to strengthen Church unity there has to be proper communication. Let's apply this requirement to relations between the Society of
Jesus and the Holy See. It's said that these relations have been
difficult in the recent past owing to poor communication. Have the
channels now been reactivated?*

I can say without fear of contradiction that today the General
Curia forms the channel for a lively and cordial bond between the
Holy See and the Society, resulting in open and loyal collaboration. This collaboration is favored notably by the tokens of encouragement and trust that the Holy Father never tires of lavish-
ing on the Society, from whose Ignatian charism he expects ever
greater service to the Church. However, the problem you raise
doesn't solely concern our relations with the Holy See, but indeed
our entire apostolic activity. For the Society to be truly of the
Church and for the Church, we have to make a greater effort to
communicate, to make the apostolic programs we're pursuing for
the good of the Church better understood. We ought, furthermore, to publicize our mode of procedure, our availability, our
hopes and our difficulties. It's a mistake to take the view that our
intentions are obvious and clear to all. If we do not make them
clearly known, the result may be that certain people will go on
thinking of the Society's activities as being parallel to the

Church's apostolate, situated on the edge of the general flow of the apostolate of the universal Church. This effort to communicate is all the more necessary in that today the great apostolic missions entrusted to us by John Paul II at the beginning of the 33rd General Congregation — from Conciliar renewal to dialogue, from inculturation to the promotion of justice — are strongly suspected, here and there, of pursuing an end contrary to that intended by the Council.

Unless I'm wrong, the suspicions are principally concerned with the practical application of the 4th Decree of the 32nd General Congregation: the one about promoting justice. We'll come back to this subject later; meanwhile can you explain what has given rise to these suspicions?

The interpretation of the decree you mention has, to quote the words of Father Arrupe, often been "mutilated, biased or unbalanced." From it has arisen an entire literature which even today, owing to selective quotations, offers a false image of the Society's physiognomy. The remarkable circulation given to this type of publication can damage the trust the Society ought to inspire if it is to succeed in its mission. Hence the need and urgency for us to make known what our true *raison d'être* in the Church and for the Church is.

How are your personal relations with the Pope?

My contacts with the Holy Father are marked by a great trust. I'm not attempting to flatter myself when I say that the Pope shows immense respect for those who work in the Church. Perhaps we don't always respond to this trust in a very responsible way.

4

A SOCIETY OF MISSIONARIES

Evangelization and respect for other cultures

How does an Order such as yours, a missionary Order from its inception, succeed in reconciling inculturation of the faith, and hence respect for the cultural values of the peoples to be evangelized, with the exigencies of Christ's command to "make disciples of all nations"?

There is always a tension between the universal commitment to make disciples of all nations and inculturation, between the proclamation of the Word of the Lord everywhere and the culture of this or that people. For us Jesuits this is forever exemplified by the case of our brother Matteo Ricci in China. Today in the Society, and I may say throughout the Church, we are deeply concerned with understanding and respecting the genuine values of the various cultures we encounter. To bear with these *might seem* to be the universal dimension of the command to convert all creatures to the Gospel. *Might seem*, since in reality inculturation is both the method and substance of true evangelization. It means encountering people in their most deeply held values, right down at their roots, and there reinforcing the meeting with the Gospel. To do this however you have to know peoples and their cultures really well, and this can reduce apostolic mobility. It's obvious, for instance, that acquiring knowledge in depth of the cultures of the people of China or of

Japan or of the Middle East, can absorb a missionary's entire lifetime, and hence it wouldn't be sensible, even for evangelistic purposes, to post a man from one country to another when he has already put in so much time in making himself a more effective apostle. Nowadays missionary mobility is at its easiest between countries that are culturally contiguous.

So it isn't true that concern over inculturating the faith has reduced the Church's missionary effort?

If we consider things in terms of numbers, in terms of the quantity of converts, it would appear that missionary effort has diminished. If on the other hand we look at the quality of the new Christians and their communities, I should say inculturation is playing an indispensable role. It was like this in the past too. I wonder, to take one example, if the speed with which the ancient Church of North Africa dissolved at the first impact with Islam wasn't due to its scant rooting in the local culture. We might also reconsider the missionary example of the Apostles themselves. From it we see they weren't primarily interested in the quantitative growth. Saint Paul was an incomparable master in this respect.

The mission in Africa

Don't you think the Churches throughout Africa may be running the same risk today as the Church of North Africa in the past? May not their over-speedy development be at the expense of a more solid rooting?

It's true these Churches have grown very quickly and this causes a number of problems. For instance, there's real difficulty in finding an adequate number of competent people to train the African clergy. But it is however also true that these Churches can count on other Churches' support and in particular that of the Church of Rome. The African Synod summoned by the Pope is only the most recent of the signs of this solidarity. I'm sure it will be a great help in seeking solutions for the main problems of the Church in Africa. The solid bond with Rome has also afforded and still affords these Churches a strong protection for their freedom in the successive political upheavals that occur in countries which have only recently gained their independence.

At times however one gets the impression that this sort of link becomes a form of control and that the African Churches are branches of the Western Churches and, in particular, of Rome.

I don't get that impression. I admit that in colonial days there were moments of great suffering for the local Churches, and also that some churchmen displayed a certain obstinacy over inculturation. Today, what may look to some people like restraining action on the part of Rome is in fact a concern to prevent the African Churches from retreating into themselves, into cultures already overtaken by the great growth of the continent. Anachronisms have to be avoided, so too the imposition of one or several cultures, those dominant ones, in areas where many different cultures are found together. The inculturation of Christianity in Africa is indeed a delicate and complex problem which won't be solved by force of slogans, nor yet by big-hearted but wild experiments. I don't think the universal Church is putting the brakes on this process, but is rather going along with it while aware of the risks it represents.

Just now you spoke of the great growth of Africa. But isn't it in fact a continent in decline, economically and socially in particular?

It's hard to speak of the whole continent. The differences between North Africa and Southern Africa for instance are obvious. It's true too there are certain facts that can't fail to alarm us.

I'm thinking, among other things, of one gigantic, scandalous fact: though living in a continent very rich in raw materials, the African peoples for the most part are still suffering from under-development. Another fact that cannot but impress us is that one African out of five is a refugee or an exile: dramatic proof that Africa has not as yet found its true stability. If on the other hand we think of all those artificial frontiers dividing it up, and that these are a legacy of colonialism, you have to hand it to the African leaders who manage to maintain relatively peaceful conditions in a situation containing all the elements required for inter-tribal massacres to explode non-stop. To complete the picture, there are ecological disasters, the advancing desert, the constant drop in price on the world market of the products of the African economy. There's material for being very pessimistic. Even so, there is, in the African peoples and in many of their leaders, a real will-to-growth which can be helped by a greater effort of international support.

The African peoples are also asking for international support so as to overcome the apartheid regime in South Africa. What is the Society's view of the system of segregation set up by Pretoria?

Jesuits who work in South Africa think the only way of overcoming apartheid is to raise the threshold of consciousness, as much of the whites as of the blacks. There we have two peoples living side by side, ignorant about one another, hating one another, and this is one of the fruits of segregation. To make people more aware, to help change minds and hearts, is the true alternative to destructive violence.

In recent decades Africa has seen a great expansion of Islam. What factors make this religion attractive to African peoples?

Rather than great I should say continuous expansion of Islam in Africa. In spite of a violent past (the Moslem Arabs were slave-traders in not a few African countries), Islam presents itself to many African cultures as a valid alternative to their own crises. Also the Islamic ethical system marks an advance over traditional African ones, without presenting the more difficult demands of Christian ethics. Also operating in favor of this expansion is the fact that, Islam not being a Church, the missionaries are the faithful themselves or certainly the faithful of the country next-door: which gives the feeling that Islam is not an imported religion.

Is African Islam fundamentalist too?

No, it's certainly more tolerant than the Arabic. An influential factor here is that, in Islamic tradition, Arabic Moslems are considered to be more truly Moslem than anyone else.

As regards evangelization, how does Islamic expansion in Africa affect the Church?

The problem arises where the Church is trying to gain a foothold among peoples still practicing their ancestral religions.

Since the spread of Islam can occur on a large scale (it only needs a tribal chief to be converted for the whole tribe quickly to become Moslems), whereas Christian evangelization is usually personal and slower, we find ourselves, objectively speaking, involved in a sort of competition over who can produce results fastest. The African Church is aware of the problem, even if it doesn't at the moment have a clear pastoral plan for dealing with it. The African Synod will certainly be discussing it, and the exchange of experiences between pastors who have attempted missionary initiatives in connection with this will be interesting.

Asia: dialogue between religions

Let's move on to the mission in Asia. In this continent, is the Church static or expanding?

On the whole I should say it's expanding. We are however talking of a Church which is a minority and sometimes a tiny minority. This fact sometimes gives rise to discouragement. For instance, it isn't uncommon in India to hear remarks like this: "After all these centuries of evangelization, Christians here barely number three per cent. Is it worth going on?" It seems to me that here people are forgetting that evangelization isn't a commercial or advertising enterprise, to be assessed on its quantitative success; on the contrary, it is witnessing to the Gospel in the midst of a people, in order to help them live a more just and human life and, if God wills, even to bring them into the Church.

Is it true that the Christians of Asia often feel like foreigners in their own countries?

Yes, since they are in fact surrounded by immense majorities practicing other religions. But you have to remember that in Asia the Christian minorities often render their countries very distinguished services, which largely offset their lack of numbers. In India, for instance, the network of Christian schools with their high level of instruction is well appreciated by the whole Indian population. In various other countries, it is the Catholic Church indeed that draws public attention to the most urgent social problems. In Thailand, it was the Church that first took steps about caring for the Cambodian refugees, thus offering a witness that impressed public opinion.

I believe one of the most interesting and delicate aspects of the mission in Asia is that of dialogue with the great religions of that continent. How does the Society contribute to this?

This was one of the great tasks entrusted to us by the Pope at the beginning of our last General Congregation, when he was pleased to meet the Jesuit delegates. The Society has always had experts on Islam, Buddhism, Hinduism and other Asiatic religions among its members. Today, perhaps we have even more of them, and it is they who are the locomotives of a dialogue which is by no means easy. One scheme which seems to enjoy a certain success, no doubt because it has the support of the Holy See, is the organizing of seminars or meetings at which bishops and spokesmen for Asiatic religions can meet to expound their respective religious beliefs and experiences. For many of them, this is the first time such a thing has happened. The program was originally launched by the Society in Taiwan and has now spread throughout Asia with results which look encouraging. In India, some Jesuits have adopted the lifestyle of Hindu monks and have set up their own ashram (monastery); it's a way of making contact easier with the people. Similar attempts are being made in Japan, by practicing Zen. In other Asian countries there are also schemes for encounter between Christian and oriental spirituality. But don't forget that in this field the most effective instrument is education in the Catholic schools, since this is the means by which non-Christians encounter Gospel values.

Not only the Lefebvrists but conservative circles in the institutional Church too have criticized the inter-religious day of prayer for peace, promoted by John Paul II at Assisi in 1986. Did this initiative, in your view, involve the risk of religious syncretism?

I think all those who took part in the day were able to see that in no way was there any risk of religious syncretism. The notion that, at Assisi, a meeting was taking place in which all religions were placed on the same level may have arisen from too-summary television and newspaper reports, unqualified by a needful explanation about what was in fact going on. This however is a risk with all forms of religious dialogue, with all ecumenism too. In this domain, I think, the people of God need to be better prepared, so as not to confuse pictures of Christian

Church leaders embracing one another with the already-achieved reunion of Christendom.

Going back to Asia . . . The Society of Jesus is expanding fast in India. What accounts for your expansion there?

The main reason is the vitality of the Catholic Church in India. Distinctions may be drawn however: for, if at one period this vitality was evident in Kerala, today it seems more so in the region of Ranchi. In any case it's a general rule: when the Church is alive, there's no lack of religious vocations.

How does this vitality of the Church in India manifest itself?

Beside the normal pastoral commitments, it is shown in its educational work and in its commitment to the very poor; and it is probably this last that attracts most young men to the religious life.

The Jesuits also have a strong presence in Japan, a country now undergoing drastic secularization. What are the affinities and differences between secularization in Japan and in the West?

I think the affinity lies only in the result. In the West, secularization has as its starting point a clearly Christian heritage, whereas the religious and cultural substratum in Japan is absolutely different.

I suppose certain aspects of secularization, such as the priority given to material values and thus to consumerism, are becoming equally widespread in Japan?

Certainly; today Japan is a very rich country, thanks to its work-ethic, something completely unknown in the Western world. We mustn't forget Japan was totally destroyed in the Second World War. Everything has been rebuilt by virtue of this work-ethic and communal labor, which seems so alien to us. I don't believe consumerism is all that widely diffused in Japan. If it were, the world economy might be better balanced: the Japanese export a lot and import very little.

In this context what are the apostolic priorities of the Society of Jesus?

The main one is education, also because it's easier to meet the Japanese in the workplace or classroom than anywhere else. Thanks to our Sophia University in Tokyo and to the network of colleges in other cities, we succeed in disseminating Christian values. And this has a certain feedback, in that each year conversions occur among our young Japanese students and some also develop vocations to the religious life.

The Society has done a lot of work in Vietnam too and is still active there. Are there any hopeful signs for the Church in Vietnam?

Yes, I think even Vietnam is on the verge of opening up. One sign of this, among others, is that several eminent Church figures have been visiting the country recently. It's to be hoped the process of opening will continue and make it possible for the Church, to which some ten per cent of the population belong, to live its own mission without interference. This would also mean recognizing religious institutes, which at present are not allowed, while a number of religious, including two Jesuits, are still in jail.

Latin America: siding with the poor

Latin America, properly speaking, isn't mission territory, since it will soon be celebrating the five hundredth anniversary of its evangelization. The Jesuits were among the first missionaries in Latin America. Are you satisfied with the Churches which your missionary zeal has brought to birth?

I ought to point out that the Jesuits were not in fact among the earliest evangelists of Latin America. They only arrived there in the sixteenth century when other religious Orders, notably the Dominicans and the Franciscans, had already put in a great deal of work. It's true however that the Society did achieve something original in Latin America, the famous *Reductions,* an apostolic experiment designed to protect the natives from a violent and ruthlessly inhumane brand of colonization. The *Reductions* were a sort of Christian republic, with features that today we regard as normal but which then were revolutionary: as for instance respect for the music and arts of native peoples, the encouragement of the laity, the organization of community life modelled on that of the earliest Christian community in Jerusalem. Alas, the political interests of Spain and Portugal snuffed out that experiment; its perceptions however are valid to this day.

Those perceptions recognized the ecclesial and social importance of the natives, a poor and oppressed people. Some twenty years ago, the Churches of Latin America recovered these perceptions by means of the option for the poor. Do the Jesuits also support this option?

They most certainly do. We ought to be thankful to Latin America for opening many people's eyes — many Jesuits' among them — to the problem of the poor. In recent years, not a few communities of the Society of Jesus have programmed their commitments on the basis of this preferential love of the poor for the Lord's sake in Latin America. This has given rise to difficulties, especially in the countries where reaction to the option has been violent and, as I have already mentioned, where a number of Jesuits have been killed due to this option.

But some Latin American Jesuits or other Jesuits who work there have been accused of following Marx rather than Christ.

Quite wrongly. They follow the example of Jesus and the teachings of the Gospel. The fact of the matter is that, in the very tense, very unjust social situation obtaining in various Latin American countries, you have only to stand up for the rights of the oppressed and work for the poor with the poor, for you to be regarded as subversives by the people who want to hang on to their own privileges and their own oppressive power.

Liberation theology

The option for the poor has come to maturity also due to a theology originating in Latin America itself: liberation theology, in the developing of which a number of Jesuits have played their part. How do you assess this theology or rather this theological current, regarded with suspicion as it appears to be by certain high Church dignitaries, as well as by the military and the ruling classes in Latin America?

First of all, one must point out that the Church has never condemned liberation theology or theologies as such. Furthermore, condemnation would be very difficult, since liberation is the basic meaning of the Passover of the Lord. Liberation is a decisively Christian event, inseparable from salvation-history. What on the other hand the Church actually has done is condemn certain aspects of some liberation theologies and precisely those ambiguous positions which threaten to reduce the Gospel message to a merely socio-cultural and political dimension, or which base liberation not on love but on class hatred. The fundamental contribution these theologies make to the ecclesial communities of Latin America is in sustaining awareness of the liberating force of the Gospel. They help provide the majority of the Latin American Churches with a rationale for enlightened pastoral policies, according to which living the true Christian life doesn't mean being resigned to conditions of abject poverty and injustice, but on the contrary means committing oneself in all seriousness to changing them for the Gospel's sake. The Gospel indeed gives us the new commandment of a love so committed as to demand the sacrifice of our own life for the good of our neighbor.

In some academic theological circles in Europe, liberation theologies are considered pretty unscientific. Is this your opinion too?

I'm not a professional theologian and so wouldn't wish to venture into fields in which I'm not competent. Certainly, the earliest works of the liberation theologians aroused a lot of criticism from European theologians over their method of theologizing and over the language they adopted, as also over their use of the Bible (particularly Exodus and the Prophets). These very criticisms addressed by European theologians to their Latin American colleagues, many of whom had completed their academic studies in Europe, served as a stimulus to refine instruments suitable for true theological reflection. Recent studies in liberation theology reveal not only the complexity and ambiguity of the various liberation theologies, but also their originality in theologizing within the very dramatic horizons of the Latin American poor. For a better understanding, I think there needs to be dialogue between European and Latin American theologians. For myself, I find the great strength of the various liberation theologies is precisely that of being close to the Christians actually engaged in liberation. Today they are making notable speculative effort, and perhaps this is necessary from a strictly theological point of view, even if there is some danger of losing contact with the poor and of becoming less effective. On the other hand, it isn't fair to expect theology to solve the problems of Latin America. Liberation theology and pastoral practice should illuminate the consciences of all Christians, particularly of those who are responsible for making decisions: politicians, economists, technologists. It is up to them to deal with the problems clear-headedly and efficiently. Convinced adherence to the Gospel will guide them to solutions taking account of the needs of the poor, in whom is Christ.

In the Churches of Latin America, conflicts frequently occur between the base and the Church hierarchy; members of religious Orders often align themselves with the base. What are the reasons for these conflicts and for the tensions between bishops and religious?

You have to distinguish between one situation and the next. In Nicaragua, for instance, there are groups of Christians who call themselves a People's Church. The name itself is tendentious for a start, in that it implies there can be one Church of the base and another one of the hierarchy; whereas there is one Church, that is to say the Lord's, in which all God's people live under the guidance of the bishops and the Pope. It is also a misrepresentation of the facts, since these groups aren't recognized by any bishop and therefore aren't ecclesial in character. Outside Nicaragua but still in Central America, it's true that in some countries there's also a lot of tension between bishops and diocesan clergy on the one hand and religious on the other. This tension sometimes manifests itself in conflicts between the Episcopal Council of Latin America (CELAM) and the Latin American Conference of Religious (CLAR). I'm sure situations of this sort have no future and that religious ought to do their best to collaborate with the whole Church. I admit the particular tasks of religious, bound as they are to the charisms of their institutes, don't always coincide with the pastoral plans of this or that local Church, but every effort ought to be made to avoid people's setting themselves up as parallel, polemical groups at odds with the hierarchy. At the same time, the hierarchy ought to recognize the scope of apostolic work, the harsh and selfless commitment to the poor, that the religious assume in Latin America. Dialogue is absolutely necessary; and it's from lack of communication that conflictual situations arise.

*A serious conflict occurred between CELAM and CLAR in 1989 over a Bible study course (*Palabra-Vida*) devised by CLAR for 1992, to mark the fifth centenary of evangelization in Latin America. Do you consider this dissension too was due to lack of communication?*

Of course it was. How could anyone think of celebrating the fifth centenary of the birth of the Church in Latin America with a program independent of the rest of the Church? That could all too easily turn into a parallel celebration. It would have shown more sensitivity if the project had been offered to the bishops, to CELAM, as a contribution towards preparing the whole Church for the fifth centenary of evangelization. Over and above the facts of this particular case, I must stress there's an absolute need in the Church to strengthen communion, the will-to-dialogue.

Five centuries of Christianity in Latin America

How should the fifth centenary of the Gospel's first being preached in Latin America be celebrated? As a festival to mark the entry of new peoples into the Church, or with a harsh examination of conscience and a spirit of penitence for the way those peoples were forced to become Christians?

As a festival in the quasi-liturgical sense: we thank the Lord for what is past and with him contemplate what is to come. I don't think any good is served by lingering over the misdeeds committed by Cortez or Pizarro. Evangelization was not conducted any differently in certain European countries. My own forefathers became Christians under the sword of Charlemagne. To say nothing of what happened later, during the Wars of Religion. In the Low Countries, the Duke of Alba massacred so many of the Dutch that even today the memory lingers on, and a mother who wants to give her child a fright says: "Look out, or I'll call the Duke of Alba!" Vladimir of Kiev behaved in just the same way, yet the Russian Church with great solemnity recently commemorated the actions of this prince who converted the Russian peoples to Christianity. To insist exclusively on the negative aspects strikes me as pretty masochistic, since you are then in danger of forgetting or undervaluing the positive ones: we think for instance of the great Dominican missionaries, Las Casas and Montesinos, to name only two, who with heroic courage defended the native populace against the cruelty of the colonists.

I might make the point that even when thinking back on events of this sort, one should bear in mind the Gospel parable of the field in which good seed and darnel grow together; the Lord himself recommends us not to be in too much of a hurry to pull up what appear to us to be weeds, lest we destroy the grain at the same time. So, let us take this commemoration of the five hundred years of evangelization as an opportunity for reflecting on how the Church in Latin America stands today with its assets and its insufficiencies, and on this basis start planning for the future.

However, there are descendants of those peoples Christianized by sword and gun, who today are keen to denounce the stifling of their own cultures.

The Church is on their side. Anyone remotely informed knows that in Latin America it's the Church above all that defends the rights of native minorities and respects their cultural values.

Various spokesmen for the Latin American Church, among them some Jesuits too, are asking that, rather than high festival, a penitential celebration be held for the fifth centenary of the preaching of the Gospel in that continent. Are they asking too much?

If it's their intention to do penance because we haven't behaved as we should, fine! This strikes me as a good suggestion. But I have a feeling that behind suggestions of this sort lurks an intention to criticize the Church, the hierarchy, who by this means could be accused *en bloc* of having been accomplices of bloodthirsty Spanish colonization. This line of criticism has been adopted by only a handful of religious who, as individuals, and notwithstanding examples set by the hierarchy, have taken the field with the oppressed. This is the thesis of the film *The Mission,* which may be a fine piece of cinema but certainly isn't an example of scrupulous historical reconstruction. A further thought: some people may be tempted to transpose what happened into present-day terms and exploit it.

How would people be able to exploit things that happened five hundred years ago?

In those people who are asking for 1992 to be an exclusively penitential celebration for the way the hierarchy behaved five hundred years ago, I seem to detect the intention of launching an implicit message about today. They tend to say that today, too, people shouldn't put much trust in the hierarchy since it is always more or less tied to the powers that be, whereas one can depend on basic communities and on everything in the Church that is of the people, since this is uncontaminated by complicity with today's oppressors. This would be as if, when we recently celebrated the two hundredth anniversary of the French Revolution, we were to have insisted on stressing only the blackest pages, the period of the Terror, while forgetting the positive contributions it made to Europe and the world in the area of the rights of man and the value of liberty.

5

POOR APOSTLES
AND PROMOTERS OF JUSTICE

Poverty for the mission

The last two General Congregations of the Society laid great stress on evangelical poverty, urging that it should be a greater feature of the life and works of the Jesuits. How has the Order responded to this?

In the reactions to the last General Congregation, I noted that many Jesuits were hoping for a more incisive prophetic voice and for the proclamation of a certain number of concrete measures to make their own daily lives and the functioning of the Society's works conform to a truly apostolic poverty. Reactions like these prove that the Society feels the urgency not only of observing the new legislation on poverty but of authentically living their apostolic mission. They prove furthermore that the Society certainly recognizes its commitment to leading a simple and austere life materially speaking, but also to expressing, in what it is and what it has, the Ignatian ideal of generosity. Though economic conditions may sometimes make this seem impracticable, Ignatian generosity can still be realized today, if there is a genuine offering of our own person, of ourselves, to help souls. Without this spirit of poverty, fully shared by those who live in our communities, the Society might appear to be a respectable un-

67

dertaking or efficient charitable organization but would no longer be proclaiming the Gospel of a poor Savior to the poor.

Does your option for the poor always have this apostolic ring to it, or do you run the risk, as some people reproach you, of becoming a body of well trained and open-hearted social workers?

I have just mentioned the great importance of Ignatian generosity and this should be able to shield us from the danger you allude to. I might add that the 33rd General Congregation of the Society neither solved all the theoretical and practical problems nor did it eliminate all ambiguities of interpretation over promoting justice in the service of the faith. The discussions on liberation theology, for their part, show how deeply the whole Church is engaged in an effort to achieve greater clarity over a matter that constitutes the object of its apostolic option. There are tensions and polarizations in our Provinces, in our communities, too. The basic incompatibility, often enough affirmed by the Church, between the priestly ministry and certain types of social commitment has created more than one deplorable and painful point of conflict. But even if these cases have caused a great stir on television and in the newspapers, we ought to remember that a much larger number of Jesuits surmount the conflict or put up with the tensions, wholeheartedly committing themselves to fight against all injustice and poverty, for the sake of the Gospel of "Blessed are the poor."

No to political or trade union militancy

To what extent is it possible for Jesuits to align themselves with the poor in the struggle for greater justice? Only to advise and encourage? Or can they take posts of responsibility in trade unions and political parties, if circumstances demand?

The answer depends on the actual situations in which this promoting of justice for the sake of the Gospel takes place. There's a whole gamut of possible scenarios here: carrying out of social projects, training of leaders, popular education, competent support for trade union activity. These are all tasks that can be performed with dramatic gestures such as hunger-strikes or publications sometimes endangering life. The way the mission of the priest workers evolved shows that, when you're promoting justice, situations can change very quickly. What does abide however is Christian love, that is to say, the love of Christ within us, for the justice willed by God for everyone. This love excludes direct political or trade union militancy for priests and religious. I would however point out that in your question there is a certain undervaluing of the roles of those who encourage or advise, roles which priests and religious can certainly discharge in these areas. It's no small thing to encourage or advise, since the aim is to educate consciences in accordance with the Gospel word; and many people would be happy if the Gospel were not to reverberate in the lives of the poor but were kept shut away in churches and sacristies. Encouraging means giving our very heart, our very life, to the task to which we are dedicated, and this doesn't strike me as inferior to direct militant activity in a party or a trade union.

If I'm not mistaken, the exclusion of priests from militant politics or trade unionism is traditionally based on the axiom that priests should be ministers of unity, not of division. But isn't it every Christian's duty to be a minister of unity? Furthermore, isn't it a bit too convenient to train and encourage members of the laity to play a militant role in a trade union or political party and then withdraw once the moment comes for concrete decisions, for putting up a fight?

Let me put the question another way. There was a time when priests and religious played a militant role in trade unions and political parties. I'm thinking for instance of the "Priest-worker movement." Gradually however the Church came to realize what the specific contribution of priests ought to be in this field. All the same it's true today that it's by no means easy, either in theory or in practice, to know where to draw the line, either because it isn't always clear where politics in the broad sense end and where party politics begin, or because the concept of party means different things, depending on whether we're talking in Europe, America or Africa. Continuous effort has to be put into clarifying exactly where the frontier should be. So, let's say, following the ancient teaching of Aristotle, that every individual is a political being and that everything the individual does or doesn't do has a political dimension. This of course applies to every Christian too.

And indeed among Christians today, the term preferred for this general political sphere governed by principles which cannot be renounced is ethics. You can't for instance be a Christian and yet stick up for apartheid. This, being an ethical rather than a political attitude, applies equally to priests. In contrast, the practical means by which apartheid is to be overcome belong to the more strictly political sphere. The Church has become aware that no priest should ever be identified with any political program or party. The main reason why doesn't have so much to do with unity as it does with the ministry of reconciliation. Once a priest lines up with one group, he excludes the others; no longer is he the man for all and no longer can he discharge the ministry of reconciliation.

But shouldn't every Christian be a minister of reconciliation?

Yes indeed, but not every Christian has the specific ministry of the priest, who acts in the name of the Lord's Church to reconcile us one to another. This is why all people of all parties should, in the priest, always be able to find the Lord in whom is our unity, our peace, our reconciliation. And this is why the Church can never take a position on the extreme wing of any movement; on the contrary, it has for the Gospel's sake to be critical of all political parties, since no party exists that can fully embody the Gospel. Since the priest represents all this, he cannot take part in politics. That doesn't mean the priest floats above the realities of this world. Not at all: he has to utter the prophetic word of the Gospel - always, everywhere. The Pope is an example of this, who certainly can't be said to be uncommitted; far from it, he's committed in all directions, not merely in one. In his most recent social encyclical *Sollicitudo rei socialis* for instance, he speaks out against both Marxist collectivism and liberal capitalism, and puts forward a concept of solidarity which, if applied to international economic politics, would radically change the world as it now is. Let me give you another example: for all extremists, the most dangerous people aren't the radicals of the opposing party, but rather the mediators. And indeed when you count up the martyrs, you'll find there are more of them among the conciliators than there are among the extremists themselves.

Couldn't a situation arise in some country which absolutely demanded the involvement of priests in parties or trade unions?

And why only in parties and trade unions? There are any number of countries in which the State for one reason or another doesn't do its duty as regards the poor. Here the Church — I mean the bishops, laity, religious, priests — can promote a multiplicity of schemes to prevent people from dying of hunger and help them to live in dignity, and yet do this without having responsibilities in trade unions or political parties.

So you veto Jesuits taking up duties in parties or unions?

Yes, I do.

Despite the fact that in exceptional cases Canon Law allows it?

Yes, and I go on doing so because I want it to be clear that involvement in a party or a trade union is not the only way of struggling with and for the poor. I further believe that in this field it is very hard to avoid ambiguity and hence I maintain it as imperative that Jesuits don't have political posts in parties or trade unions.

So, if Jesuits take on political posts because in conscience they feel they ought to do so, they have no alternative but to leave the Society?

Yes, this was exactly what happened in Nicaragua with a Jesuit who was obliged to leave the Society because he couldn't in conscience see his way to leaving his post as Minister of Education in the Sandinista government. Earlier, when Father Arrupe was General, there was the case of a Canadian Jesuit who became a minister in the Quebec government. When his appointment was over, he was keen to rejoin the Society and now he's a missionary in Madagascar where he's doing a great job promoting better conditions for the poorest of the poor in Antananarivo.

But when Father Cardenal had to leave the Society in Nicaragua, didn't you write him a letter expressing sympathy over the priest/minister's conscience-inspired choice?

Yes, and I'd do it again. I can certainly understand the reasons a conscientious objector may have, but he cannot claim the right to impose his reasons of conscience on the institution against which he is objecting.

And yet you maintain that conscientious objection is still possible within the Church?

One can't discuss this in the abstract. In the case of a few priests who have maintained, precisely on grounds of conscience, that they ought to go on serving the poor in a government post, it seems to me the answer is yes. At the same time, they have loyally accepted the Church's rule imposing suspension from the priestly ministry on anyone discharging a political or governmental function. From the moment they were deprived of the right of celebrating Mass and the other sacraments, they abstained from celebrating them. Hence, what we have here, rather than a conscientious objection against the Church, is a conscientious choice between Church ministry and a commitment to improving the condition of the poor, expressed within a strictly political context.

The whole Society for the promotion of justice

Let's turn to the entire Society's commitment in this field. It was established during the 32nd General Congregation that the promotion of justice ought to be the concern of all Jesuits, but in some sectors of the Order there was resistance to this. The 33rd General Congregation changed the terminology, speaking of preferential love for the poor, and the opposition seems to have died down. Was it only a matter of wording?

Quite so, and it does perhaps seem rather peculiar that the 32nd General Congregation's 4th Decree no longer encounters the resistance it aroused on being published ten years before. Some Provincial Superiors have told me they don't feel entirely comfortable over the way, after the position adopted by the 33rd General Congregation on preferential love of the poor, the Jesuits admitted a bit too easily that they'd been wrong over that choice. Since it was affirmed at the last General Congregation that not only some members of the Society but all its works were to be subsumed into promoting justice for the Gospel's sake, possibly some Jesuits thought this had been done already; whereas the work that lies ahead is extremely hard and still all has to be done. I recognize that the promotion of justice now preoccupies the

attention of all Jesuits and that, even if the practice doesn't always
tally with the ideal, everyone is aware that in the Society today
there is no longer any possibility of deciding to open or to close a
house, to renovate or to leave things as they are, without taking
the promotion of justice for the Gospel's sake into account.

*Was the Society's decision to commit itself more completely to
the promotion of justice a choice arrived at calmly?*

I have to confess that during the 32nd General Congregation
I sat open-mouthed. I arrived from the Middle East to find myself
immersed in a set of problems I had never even heard of: neither
the expression promotion of justice nor all sorts of similar ones
were known to me. And yet I had been living among the destitute
in Egypt and in other extremely precarious situations in other
Middle Eastern countries. It must be said that the Society was
then exclusively orientated towards traditional forms of apostolate and, to alter that state of affairs, everything had to be pushed
to the point of exaggeration in the opposite direction. It was a fact
that after the 32nd General Congregation not a few Jesuits felt the
Society was, practically speaking, split into two sectors of work:
the section for promoting justice, which was the sector of the
future, and the sector for traditional work, which was doomed to
disappear. Even today there are some Provinces where tensions
of this sort exist, as though the Society were incapable of dealing
with both sectors at once. But in the Society as a whole we are
truly aware that any work the Lord entrusts to us has to be deeply
permeated with an eager desire to promote justice for the
Gospel's sake.

*To reach agreement, it was sufficient to alter one expression:
from "promotion of justice" to "preferential love for the poor"?*

Despite the diversity of opinions on the matter, preferential
love for the poor isn't an expression attenuating the other, even if

some Jesuits believe that, under the new formula, love for the poor is less demanding, more religious and less "threatening." The word love can equally well mean sympathy or charitable work as it can a commitment strong as death. But in current usage, justice seems to denote a more demanding challenge. I therefore think we ought to stay faithful to the expression "promotion of justice." Father Arrupe loved to repeat: "You can't bring about justice without love. And you can't stop loving when you're fighting injustice since, for Christ, to love all is a commandment admitting of no exception." Just as the proclamation of the faith, from the very beginnings of the Society, has been inseparable from the proclamation of justice, so love and justice must never be separated. Justice bears on those concrete realities where what human beings need to be truly human is lacking, and thus on the social and economic facts of life.

Do you believe that the teaching of the Church can produce an effect on concrete problems in the social and economic spheres?

The concept of justice being realistic, as understood by Christianity, cannot ignore the real, concrete problems of our times: problems are all too often attributed to fatally unjust structures in our society when in fact they are due to a human liberty of which unjust use is being made. To the reality of injustice the reality of the promotion of justice should correspond: a justice claimed not on one's own behalf but, for the Gospel's sake, on behalf of others, of the victims of injustice and of those who have no voice. What perhaps wasn't clear when the 32nd General Congregation's already cited 4th Decree was written but has become progressively clearer in application is the close link that exists between socio-economic justice on the one hand, with all the human rights that this involves, and on the other with the justice of God which, by transforming our hearts, lays a foundation for all human justice.

The difficult role of the Social Centers

Scattered throughout the world, your Social Centers are particularly committed to the promotion of justice. How do these Social Centers work? Is it true that in some regions they have been in danger of causing rifts in the Society and, more generally, in the Church?

During the initial period of applying the decree on the promotion of justice, and of the activity of the Social Centers, mistakes were made, some of them grave. In the cause of proclaiming justice, which has to be done in serving the faith, here and there the actual service of the faith and the centrality of the faith were forgotten about. The absolute need for a concrete connection between the two ends, faith and justice, was obstructed either by difficulties encountered in reorienting various ministries and in identifying the services that justice required, or by a serious crisis of faith. Similar crises of faith still have repercussions today in the concrete manifestations of a religious life that sometimes seems to have lost its proper roots in Gospel witness and to have as though exhausted the prophetic vigor of its vocation in the Church and for the Church.

What people accuse your Social Centers of in point of fact aren't religious deviations but left-wing political choices.

True, some people maintain that the Society's Social Centers haven't been able to develop a truly effective action owing to the lack of a precise and clear socio-political option. By decisively opposing capitalistic choices, the Centers have oriented themselves towards the positions of the forces of the left with no intention of allying themselves or identifying themselves with unacceptable Marxist programs, yet sympathizing with forms and expressions proper to Marxism. Viewed with suspicion by the right and not accepted, actually, by the left, they or some of them at least have finished up finding themselves stranded halfway between two shores. Some of them haven't dared to repudiate their unacceptable Marxist orientation fairly and squarely, for fear of losing contact with the left. Yet they hesitate to adopt the Church's criteria for evangelical discernment in social questions and come out openly in favor of the known social doctrine of the Church, a teaching which contains guidelines, directives and the positions to be adopted on determined problems.

Can there be only opposition between the Church's social teaching and Marxism?

Their strategic and tactical methods being radically opposed, Church and Marxism can only battle against one another in confrontation and mutual distrust. For us Jesuits it's of primary importance to hang on to Father Arrupe's teaching on Marxist Analysis. Having stressed how hard it is, if not impossible, to divorce the Marxist analysis from Marxist ideology to which it is connected, he concluded with these words: "I ask you all to conduct yourselves with crystalline clarity and faithfulness. I beg you to commit yourselves with all your energy, in harmony with your vocation, in favor of the poor and against injustice, without however allowing indignation to darken your vision of faith, and always maintaining, even in the fire of conflict, a Christian demeanor characterized by love and not by hardness of heart."

Since the gates of capitalism, as indeed those of Marxism, are closed, where better than in the Church's teaching to seek guidelines for research work, projects, theories and undertakings, and thus confer on the activities of the Social Centers a politico-social direction true to themselves? Indeed, definite lines of advance are now beginning to emerge. Even if you can't say Marxism is dead, there's no doubt Marxism-Communism is in crisis. Wouldn't it be tragic if its last, irreducible supporters were actually to be the religious?

Can you give me any example of the new lines of advance now emerging?

Some Jesuits have been in a position to offer a valid contribution towards the detailed application of the pastoral letter *Economic Justice for All* issued by the bishops of the United States. This is one example of what the Church expects of us: not that we confine ourselves merely to repeating what the Magisterium has taught us, but that we contribute to developing it later and to guaranteeing its vitality. It is our duty to participate in the task of deepening the theological dimension of such statements by the Magisterium and of assuring their dynamism as sources of inspiration and guidance, just as a number of Bishops' Conferences have succeeded in doing. As people competent in the social sciences, attentive and sensitive to the cry of the poor, the Jesuits who work in the Social Centers are well placed to enrich the Church's teaching with those mediating factors required for it to maintain its place within the historical channel of social reality.

You are well aware the Jesuits' Social Centers have been accused of engaging in politics. On the other hand, how can one not engage in politics when one is committed to transforming society?

It's a fact, when we talk about a Social Center's activity, inevitably politics are involved. In this field, where everything can easily take on a political complexion, we should avoid operating as though everything resolved itself into politics. We have to do this, since for us believers promoting social justice is rooted in proclaiming the faith. Hence our preoccupation with the poorest of the poor can never be motivated and guided by the conviction that the adequate response to the exigencies of the situation are exclusively political. Consequently, a Jesuit is required not to be the exponent of the politics of a given party, not to be someone who acts on behalf of an institution or of an ideology. This is extremely difficult behavior to maintain, since a Social Center can't carry out its functions without keeping in contact with the political realities and without accepting responsibility for the research it conducts about institutions, ideologies and political parties. It isn't possible clearly to define the criteria to be observed in undertakings connected with activities and institutions that have an undeniably political dimension. Be that as it may, a Jesuit should in every situation bear witness to the spiritual and historical tension that exists between the importance and the insufficiency of political action; a Jesuit should be interested in people not so much and not only because they are poor in the economic and social sense but because they are made in the image of God: brothers and sisters of Christ and children of the Father.

The Jesuits and Italian politics

I should like to direct the conversation to a very specific situation, that of the Istituto Pedro Arrupe *in Palermo, where the Jesuits have founded a school of political education which seems to have given offense to several political parties and various Catholic movements into the bargain. What do you think of the criticisms levelled against this undertaking of your Order?*

I entirely agree with what Father Federico Lombardi, Provincial of the Italian Jesuits, has had to say about it. The school of political education in Palermo came into being in response to two demands, the one ecclesial, the other historical. The ecclesial demand is the growth among Italian Catholics of a more informed awareness of having to bear witness to the Gospel in dealing with the crucial questions of our age. The historical demand derives from the debate over a number of important problems which have been bedeviling Italian society for years: the party system and its infiltration of every aspect of society; the moral question which concerns not only the honesty of politicians but the corruption endemic in the functioning of the very institutions of the State; the institutional question, that is to say, the relationship between society and the State. To deal with these demands, the Jesuits of Palermo rightly felt it their duty to respond in the best tradition of the Order and in line with the Synod on the Apostolate of the Laity: I mean, with an educational proposal. A proposal inspired by one or two essential ideas: first and foremost, the idea of the common good as lodestone of political activity; then, the need for competence and for ways of acquiring it. The fact that the Palermo school is only one of many founded on the initiative of dioceses and other ecclesial entities in Italy before or since goes to show there was a real demand for training centers of this sort.

And yet the school of Fathers Sorge and Pintacuda in Palermo has been the only one to provoke so much resentment in one sector of Italian politics that one party secretary has defined it as "a school for trouble-makers." How is this kind of reaction to be explained?

As a guest in Italy, my mother's family's native land, I can't hold forth on the reactions of Italian political parties. All I can say, again agreeing with Father Lombardi, is that in this, as in analogous initiatives of the Jesuits, there is no hidden design to direct the political game in any particular direction, even though the Jesuits in Palermo, as elsewhere, have the right and duty to take up supportive or critical positions, according to circumstance, with regard to those who, above all in the more difficult social situations, emit signals or act in ways that help or block the just development of the human community.

How do you react when the Italian press, and sometimes not only the Italian, writes about Jesuit policy?

I don't lose my cool, for a start. Here I think we're dealing with malicious generalizations, since it surely must be common knowledge that there's no such thing as a Jesuit policy. There are, conceivably, Jesuits who write about politics, but when they do so they certainly aren't expounding a political line of the Society's. They're simply doing their job as chroniclers or political commentators. Take the case of *Civiltà Cattolica*. Every fortnight the Italian press notes the political comments of this review and ascribes them generically to the Jesuits, whereas everyone knows that *Civiltà Cattolica* is in fact a periodical traditionally much closer to the Holy See than to the General Curia of the Society, without being actually a mouthpiece, either official or unofficial, of the Vatican. This said, I can guarantee that no one Jesuit political policy exists; as far as political opinions go however, I believe there may be about twenty-five thousand, one (that is to say) for every member of the Society.

Joking apart, are you in favor of political pluralism for Catholics?

Generally speaking, I should say yes, but one must take the actual situations in different countries into consideration. It isn't out of the question, for instance, that in Italy the episcopate may think it necessary, to safeguard Gospel values, for Catholics to be under one political roof. In contrast, it's possible that in other countries the episcopates, owing to different political situations, may not be concerned about this.

Do you think the adjective "Christian" applied to a party or other secular organization may give rise to misunderstandings by involving the religious dimension in the ambiguities of politics?

Misunderstandings are always possible but I don't think one ought to erect this into a principle, otherwise we should have to drop the adjective "Catholic" from all our schools, universities, hospitals, and social centers, etc., in a word from all those entities that are, at bottom, attempts to embody the Gospel on earth. The Gospel is, yes, a sublime message, but it has to be translated into practical terms. I don't see why there should be no reference to Christian values in our works, and I don't exclude it either with regard to political movements that draw their inspiration from the Gospel. But for a party or movement to describe itself as "Christian" entails a great responsibility and postulates a personal and communal witness of total adherence to Gospel inspiration.

6

TEACHERS OF LIBERATION

A thousand schools of higher education

The last two General Congregations of the Society of Jesus stated that the promotion of justice occupies first place in your apostolic mission. How do you manage to harmonize this priority with the other commitments — to take education first — which still occupy a pretty large number of Jesuits?

The educational sector is, numerically speaking, the most important one in the Society. We are at this moment responsible for upwards of a thousand institutes of higher education. I'm convinced the promotion of justice by our Order can't be effective unless the educational sector is increasingly committed to this mission. The 32nd General Congregation's Decree 4 is in line with this, despite the fact that there may have been mistaken interpretations of it. It asks that the Jesuit apostolate in the field of education be increased and stresses the importance of training multiplying agents, that is to say, those who can act in such a way as to change the attitudes of individuals and the unjust structures of society. Be it said, too, that what is now being put in question is certainly not our commitment in the field of education, but rather the way in which it is integrated into our mission. I remember Father Arrupe loved to repeat that the aim of our activity in this field is to train men for others. So there's no conflict between the educational apostolate and the promotion of justice.

But this is all rather vague. What concrete steps are you taking to adjust your work in the educational field to the promotion of justice?

We are making a serious effort in this direction. Some Provinces have taken very far-reaching decisions and are facing grave difficulties in order to remain faithful to their commitments. I could certainly mention concrete examples, at university or college level, that go beyond fine initiatives which sometimes have little effect, such as grants for study or travel to discover the real facts about a country. I should however point out that, when dealing with education, it is particularly important and effective to introduce the promotion of justice into the disciplines being taught. And this is being done for instance in many of our secondary schools in North and South America, in East Asia and in India. In the course of the last five years, a well thought out and comprehensive program has been started in these regions to encourage students to think about the relationship between the promotion of justice and the sciences, the arts, history, sociology, philosophy and religious culture itself. In not a few of our universities too, seminars take place on human rights, economics, politics, ecology, and research projects are being introduced on the causes of poverty, discrimination and other phenomena of the sort. We can already see the effectiveness of programs of Christian service, putting students into direct contact with the lives and problems of the poor, the aged, the handicapped, the marginalized. By means of personal contact and reflection on these experiences, we hope to motivate our students to correct unjust conditions. As you see, a lot is being done; but of course there's still a great deal more to do.

Do you think it possible to educate for liberation by teaching biology or engineering? Isn't there a risk of "voluntarism" in the scientific and technological sectors which in themselves are neutral?

All disciplines can be taught and studied with a view to integral human liberation. It's generally known today, it seems to me — and certainly among the Jesuits — that no teaching is neutral, and that every teacher, whether instructing in mathematics or politics, literature or philosophy, is a vehicle for values which may be in harmony or in conflict with the promotion of justice and hence with the Gospel message. At the moment, genetic engineering is developing in a surprising way. This development can't be regarded as a simple laboratory fact, since the enormous implications for the future of the human race cannot but raise the fundamental question: merely because a thing is possible, should it automatically be done? The problem of values ought to be an integral part of any intelligent research in the field of genetic engineering, if the aim is to train competent and responsible people.

Promoters of justice or defenders of the "status quo"?

Rather than educating the young for the promotion of justice or for a preferential love for the poor, your colleges and universities seem geared to train them for being top professional people and very much members of the society in which they live. Isn't there a risk here of endorsing the preservation of the "status quo"?

I'm convinced that in four hundred years of history our educational institutions have had as their sole end the commitment to make the human city a more just one for the Lord's sake. I'm anxious to emphasize this since, when we Jesuits declare that today we are called to promote justice and to live the option for the poor, we aren't formulating a new response; it is rather a new way of expressing an old response, well anchored in our Jesuit traditions. We have never been satisfied with mere cultural transmission. We have always insisted on developing a critical attitude, to equip our students to contribute to human and cultural

growth and to renewal in harmony with Gospel values. Especially
during periods when society is undergoing major transformation,
such as our own, there is always the urgent need to renew social
structures by bringing into being the new creation offered us by
Jesus Christ who was himself profoundly committed to justice, to
reconciliation, to truth, to the needs of the poor, to compassion,
to everything that, in the spirit of the Beatitudes, the Father wills
that we too should practice. Indeed, the concern for justice is no
new element in our educational activity. Ignatius wanted the
earliest Jesuit colleges to be open to all and completely free of
charge. The *Ratio Studiorum* of 1599 enjoins teachers to take
particular pains over poor students.

*Such were the fine schemes or good resolutions of the early
days. Can you honestly say that things are still like that? That the
Society's colleges and the other educational institutions you run give
preference to the poor?*

First of all I'd like to make the point that you can't really talk
about "fine schemes or good resolutions of the early days," given
that Saint Ignatius's original scheme of giving a free education in
our colleges lasted for more than two hundred years, until the
suppression of the Society in 1773. Each college had to have a
"foundation," given by a private benefactor, or by the city or
community desiring to have a college opened. In cases where a
"foundation" still existed, the same free education was re-
continued in the nineteenth century with the restoration of the
Society of Jesus which occurred in 1815, and this went on until
modern states confiscated the property of the colleges in question. In Italy, for instance, this happened with the fall of Rome in
1870. At present, the disagreement over free education in our
colleges, and in our academic educational institutions in general,
is a problem common to all Catholic schooling. This said, I should
like to make it clear that the option for the poor is not exclusive
nor, even less, based on class distinctions. The option for the

poor doesn't mean — sticking to the field of education — that we Jesuits should dedicate ourselves solely to the neediest of boys and young men. The option is actually more comprehensive, more demanding, and requires us to train everyone — rich, poor, middle classes — in the perspective of justice, that is to say, in the universal, catholic horizon of salvation history. It means, in other words, teaching the young of every social class to grow in Christ's special love for the poor.

And how do you do this?

It's a general orientation: interest in social problems has to be explicitly present in our colleges and universities. We Jesuits furthermore have to act in such a way that each of our students takes the option for the poor as the criterion of his or her own education and of the choices to be made later in life. And that, I ought to hammer home once again, not for any class choice dictated by fashion, but for an exquisitely evangelical necessity. Training students of every socio-economic class to acquire a permanent state of mind leading them never to take an important decision without having first weighed its consequences for the poor means being committed to training men and women for others, with Christ as their model.

Obstacles to Catholic education

To have free colleges again, as Ignatius wanted, you would need people to finance them. Who could be the new Maecenas today?

Today the new Maecenas would have to be the State, whether because our schools, and Catholic education in general, perform a public service, or as a matter of justice. It isn't in fact fair that parents who send their children to private schools should have to pay twice over for an educational service to which their children have a right: they pay for State education out of their taxes and private education out of their own pocket. Since in many parts of the world the State doesn't take this view, we and other religious institutes committed to scholastic education are forced to ask the families of our pupils for financial help, for us to be able to cope with the huge expenses involved in the running of a school. Because of this, we know that some of our schools are only available to the rich and hence offer an image of class privilege, but we are forced to do this. We should like to expand our educational commitment to the neediest families much more, and I must say that, wherever we can, we are taking positive steps to do so. For instance, the Jesuit secondary schools and universities in North America have been working hard over the last twenty-five years to collect funds from benefactors and to found free schools for poor students. Every year now, tens of millions of dollars are made available to guarantee teaching, registration fees, books and so forth for students from poor families. We Jesuits sympathetically salute all initiatives aimed at parity of financial support for State schools and non-State schools, the latter being incorrectly called private. Having made these points, if we take our work in the educational field as a whole, free schooling is a significant aspect of it, since we certainly aren't working to show a profit.

What is your position over improved working conditions won by school staffs and does it also apply to private institutions?

I'm glad about the improvements school staffs have managed to obtain. I should however add that, since the mission of the Catholic schools demands a total devotion to the teaching of Gospel values by word and deed, teachers in these schools have to be evaluated on the strength of this criterion, as well as from the strictly academic and professional point of view. Their continuous service in the Catholic schools exacts a constant contribution to the specific mission characterizing them.

Apart from economic difficulties and perplexities to do with labor relations, what other obstacles do your educational institutions encounter today?

Owing to the way that science has developed and to other external factors, we are ever less able to control study programs, which ought to be transmitting values, proclaiming the Word of God and making it possible for students to share the vision generated by the Christian faith. In some countries this is due in part to government controls affecting the content of the curriculum. The tendency, too, to specialize in different fields risks becoming a travesty of true education by depriving it of any coherence. Catechesis is thrust to one side and reduced to one brief hour of religious instruction. Owing to our decrease in numbers, if we go on calling on the Jesuits merely as spiritual directors, to give a Christian orientation and atmosphere to our colleges, there will be a serious weakening of this dimension of the Ignatian mission. True, in a certain number of countries we have been working for more than ten years now at sharing the Ignatian spiritual and educational tradition with our lay colleagues and some notable progress has been achieved, but there's still a lot that needs to be done.

Do your pupils' families always share your educational ideals?

We do meet one or two obstacles from this quarter. For instance, while I can perfectly well understand the resistance of people who merely want a sound academic and professional education for their sons, what I find absolutely impossible to grasp is the attitude of those who oppose the promotion of justice, as though it were an ideological derivative of Marxism, and who see the option for the poor as a betrayal of the traditional Jesuit vocation, viewed as a commitment to train an elite whose power is based on knowledge and possessions. This is even harder to understand when we consider the teachings of the Church. Long before the Second Vatican Council and with growing insistence over more recent years, the Church, in the name of the Gospel, has been proclaiming the right of every human being to his or her own personal dignity and to the exercise of personal liberty, and has been demanding the elimination of everything preventing people from becoming fully themselves.

How do you contrive to preserve the identity of the Society's colleges and universities when faced with the problems you have just been mentioning?

Our educational institutions make their essential contribution to society by striving to make a rigorous and honest study of the world's most crucial problems. Hence the Society's colleges and universities have to be distinguished by their high academic qualities. We aren't interested in finding answers to problems inspired by ideologies, by fashions or by over-simplifications. The teaching, the research and everything else to do with the educative process are elements of the greatest importance in our institutions, precisely because we reject any partial or distorted vision of the human person. This is in clear contrast to those educational institutions that ignore the human person owing to their fragmented approach to problems or to an excessive specialization.

Pastoral activity and schooling

I suppose that, besides a proper concern for professionalism, your educational institutions are meant to be distinguished for a specifically pastoral dimension. How do you manage to achieve this objective?

The fully Christian and human vision guiding our educational policy favors the pastoral dimension of the work we do in our colleges and universities. Let us take the by no means simple problems facing men and women in the closing years of the twentieth century. No academic discipline can legitimately claim to provide exhaustive answers to the questions raised by genetic research, the origin and purpose of human life, urban planning, poverty, illiteracy, technological developments in the medical or military field, human rights, environment, computers. All this no doubt requires a mass of empirical data and technological knowledge, but equally demands that the effects the proposed solutions may have on the deepest essence of men and women be not overlooked. In other words, the solving of these problems requires that we do not overlook the sociological, psychological, ethical, philosophical and theological dimensions. To sum up, solving these gravest of human problems requires us to be open to the widest and deepest aspects of the human personality, with an inter-disciplinary effort that ignores no aspect of that personality.

I understand the need for all disciplines to be keyed together but what has this got to do with the pastoral dimension of your more than one thousand colleges and universities?

What indeed! No research into the total human condition can leave the Christian experience aside. This is all the truer for the Society's educational institutions, since these are inspired by the deep conviction that God made himself human in Christ in order to divinize human nature. The specific motivation of our educational work to promote human welfare has its source of inspiration and its ultimate criterion in the mystery of Christ. To echo a thought dear to Father Karl Rahner, Christology is the starting point and completion of anthropology; Christology is anthropology fulfilled. Perhaps it will be clearer if we clinch this same theological concept with what Saint Paul wrote, where he described Christ as "the new man" (Ep 2:15), "the perfect man" (Ep 4:13). On the same theological line of thought about anthropology as being founded in and commensurate with Christology, the Second Vatican Council, in the Constitution *Gaudium et spes* (n. 22), made a highly significant statement: in fact only in the mystery of the Incarnate Word does the mystery of human nature find true light . . . Christ, who is the new Adam, by himself revealing the mystery of the Father and his love, so too reveals human nature to the human race and makes us aware of our most exalted vocation: to become children of God in Christ Jesus. Now the transfiguration of Christ by the work of the Spirit is part of human reality. This transfiguration is constantly going on among us, saving us and calling on us individually to integrate it into our consciousness. This transfiguration, this saving power, is what transforms a Jesuit's educational work into an adventure at once human and divine. Let me add one concrete fact: in many of our secondary schools and not a few universities, groups have been set up to provide a pastoral ministry to complement the religious instruction given under the official syllabus. These groups deal with the students' liturgical and sacramental life, organize spiritual retreats and offer the possibility of spiritual direction and advice on religious matters.

We shall never give up teaching

About eight thousand Jesuits are occupied in teaching, that is, a third of the Society's members. Aren't the decrease in vocations and the contemporary calls on Jesuits for other activities going to force you to shed some of your educational institutions?

Sooner or later, I believe, we shall have to close some colleges and entrust other people with the responsibility for a certain number of our educational institutions. But our teaching apostolate has to go on, integrating itself ever more completely into the process of renewal through which we are living. This renewal has already helped the Society to become aware of one pretty elementary truth, though one which many Jesuits have a job to admit: we are not the only people capable of giving Ignatian inspiration to an institution belonging to the Society. This conviction has stimulated our commitment over the past ten years to training our lay colleagues in Ignatian spirituality. In this connection and with some satisfaction, I'm watching the positive results of the *Colloquium on the Ministry of Teaching,* a fruitful initiative intended to encourage lay and Jesuit teachers to reflect and pray together and share their thoughts about teaching, understood as a ministry of the Church and of the Society. The *Colloquium* and its subsequent developments have so far been adopted by the Jesuit schools in thirty-three countries. In some of our universities as well, frequent seminars on Ignatian spirituality for teachers have become a normal feature of campus life. This is a lesson we should also try to apply in relationships between the Society and its former pupils. Looking at the problem another way, I should like to refer once more to Saint Ignatius, who towards the end of 1543 founded the House of Saint Martha in Rome for the rehabilitation of prostitutes. He saw the importance of this type of work but resolved to let other people run it, once it had been properly started. This is a spirit frequently manifesting itself in Ignatius's life. Not that he wanted to abandon the works once they were launched; but rather that he thought the Society's mission should be discharged with the full participation and collaboration of other people. The unusual expression used by Father Arrupe: "We should train multiplying agents" derives from this same vision of Ignatius. Ignatius's correspondence, consisting of 6,815 letters, demonstrates brilliantly how he never stopped seeking and encouraging the fullest collaboration with every sort of person: princes and poor people, people of culture and businessmen, working men and university professors.

Don't you think the urgency of other tasks might require the Society to abandon the teaching apostolate altogether?

No, the Society could never dissociate itself from the teaching apostolate, although the forms of this may change. To give up our apostolate as teachers would be to give up evangelization, since it is precisely by means of education — at home and at school — by means of teaching and by means of the personal attention they get that children and young people lay the foundations for their future. To become fully mature, a person has to undergo a process in which others, above all teachers, intervene as being qualified to help the individual develop the whole spiritual, intellectual and emotional potential hitherto latent. To neglect education means giving up the possibility of building a future for an individual, a people, a nation; it means giving up the possibility of releasing all the loving energy of a human being, whose future happiness and maturity depend on the degree to which one arrives at being what one is in the depths of oneself: a child of God. This is so essential a task that helping souls would be an empty phrase were it not embodied in one way or another in the teaching apostolate.

The Ignatian method of teaching

Four centuries of educational activity, hundreds of schools of every kind, thousands, indeed millions, of alumnae: the Society can certainly be proud of the great part it has played in education. Where do your teaching methods come from? Is there an Ignatian method?

I should say yes, and I think it can be deduced from the central idea of Ignatian spirituality. This is born of the loving encounter of an actual person, Ignatius of Loyola, with the Father's love, breaking into human history by means of another real person, Jesus of Nazareth. This encounter is illuminated and guided by study of the Gospel, or rather by Ignatius's particular reading of the Gospel. He interprets his own life as surrender to a cause and, in the light of this interpretation, he reads the Gospel. In it he encounters a God, the man-God Jesus, who has not only dedicated his own life to the cause of the Father and humankind, but calls other human beings to follow him. Round this central idea the whole Ignatian vision is organized: a vision of God as a merciful and faithful Father who intervenes in human history; a positive vision of the world as place for the personal encounter between the individual and God as Father, though not ignoring the weight of evil from which we all need to be freed; a positive vision of humanity, summoned to freedom and summoned to take up the burden of returning the world to God. At the center of this dynamic vision stands the person of Jesus, the Master, calling us. Ignatius was a great lover of Christ and his cause.

From this religious, indeed Catholic, vision, what pedagogic guidelines can you derive?

We derive notions perfectly grasped by Ignatius and applied by him in the field of the educational apostolate: the great stress laid on freedom; the positive value accorded to the world and particularly to culture; the response to the call of Jesus, which may not be a self-centered response but demands that we be and teach others to be, in Father Arrupe's words, men for others. Ignatius insisted on the need for discernment, understood as a means of getting to know God's will, and in our schools and universities reflection and discernment are regarded and adopted as characteristic pedagogic methods. It seems to me, this spirituality and this method of teaching, demanding and time-consuming though they may be, are deeply contemporary. They make us confident that we can genuinely satisfy the needs of today's young people as they seek to give a sense of completeness to their lives, as they seek values for which it is worth the effort to commit themselves, as they become ever more aware of their dignity and of their freedom.

How are, or how would you wish, the Jesuits' former pupils to be?

The Society hopes its former pupils will be socially recognizable as such, not only or not mainly by certain traits most easily specified — competence, qualifications — but by their commitment to the service of fundamental Christian and human values. It would like them to be mature personalities, rich in kindness, and anxious to commit themselves to the cause of true justice or to the generous service of the people of God. The Society would like its former pupils to be the living expression, in whatever environment they may find themselves, of the pedagogic ideals that I've just been describing.

Jesuits and the mass media

Don't you think today the multiplying agents are also to be found in the mass media? What initiatives has the Society taken in this sector?

As a whole, the Society perhaps discovered this sector rather late in the day and consequently doesn't have a great many men trained to work in the mass media. To make up for lost ground, Father Arrupe founded *Jescom,* an organization to coordinate and help Jesuits working in this sector, and an Institute, with its seat in London, to train Jesuits and other Christians who intend to involve themselves in the modern means of social communication. I think that, generally speaking, there's a growing awareness in our Order of the educational and pastoral importance of these means and consequently we now envisage an introduction to the use of these instruments as part of the training of Jesuits in the future. In our universities too, including the Gregorian, we now have research centers dealing with the mass media.

And from the point of view of actually doing things, what is going on?

At present, the Society is making a special effort in the use of radio, which is of the utmost importance for popular education, specially in Latin America. A fair number of Jesuits are working on training programs for TV, also in countries in the East. Then there's the vast field of periodicals, in which Jesuits have been active for a long while, though here we're talking mainly about publications of interest to specialists, not properly speaking about mass media. I should also mention that several Jesuit universities run Departments of Communication, which train graduates and non-graduates in the production techniques of the mass media (TV, cinema, radio, press, etc.) and offer other specialized courses in visual instruction, in the communication of values in and through the media, etc.

Some of your periodicals are sometimes pretty scathing in their treatment of pastoral problems. I'm thinking of the French Etudes, The Month *in England and* America *in the United States. Do you occasionally have to intervene to tone down the critical spirit of these magazines?*

Frankly, no, since these and other magazines are within the primary competence of their respective Provinces, not of the General government of the Society. I should like to stress however that a periodical belonging to the Society isn't allowed to be systematically critical in a negative way about the Church's hierarchy. This doesn't mean that no critical articles may be published. The important thing is, by analogy with what I was saying earlier when we were discussing the relationship between theological research and the Magisterium, that the criticism be set in a context such that all the elements of the problem in question are fairly presented and, hence, that the hierarchy's position is also correctly reported. These journals deal with many difficult topics and ought to help the people of God to get their bearings, by presenting them with every aspect of a given problem. It's clear that the voice of the Magisterium isn't one voice among many: it has a unique authority. In this field, there are two elements that seem to me important: the competence of the writer, which should be such as to furnish a complete treatment in depth, and the tone of the article, which should never evince an aggressive spirit but rather a determination to present the deeper meaning of events.

Criticism as contribution to the search for truth, you say. This is fine in other fields, particularly in that of scientific research. In your more than one thousand seats of learning, comprising universities and institutes of higher education, do you always succeed in reconciling academic freedom with faithfulness to the teachings of the Church?

Contrary to the commonly held notion that the Church limits academic freedom, I'm convinced the Church protects and stimulates this freedom by proposing fundamental questions about human nature for research. Research runs the risk of following the thrust of scientific interest alone, but human beings are more important than science; the true end of science is the human being, human welfare. Today there is a growing awareness among scientists that human values are involved in all research. Even economics are never scientific in the abstract; in application they invariably concern human beings, their values, their social relations. The Church supports this growing awareness in the field of scientific research and calls on scientists not to involve themselves in research that can produce dehumanizing results. Perhaps this isn't always immediately clear, but sooner or later it becomes so. For instance, the encyclical *Humanae vitae,* and the Instruction of the Congregation for the Doctrine of the Faith *Donum vitae,* regarded by many people as repressive documents, are in fact trying to protect, in the former one, human love and, in the latter, human life. Besides, certain documents issued by the Holy See often stress what they are trying to limit, without giving the reasons for such limitations, deeply humane though they are.

Do you think this line is always followed in Jesuit universities?

There may be a conflict of ideas from time to time, but the Society will always ask every institute for which it is responsible to be loyal and respectful towards the Magisterium.

7

NEW COMMITMENTS

In the Church and in the world

In days gone by the Jesuits were known as the Pope's Praetorian Guard. *You were in the vanguard of all battles in defense of the Church and particularly of the Roman Pontiff. In recent decades and above all since the Second Vatican Council, you seem to have been undergoing a profound transformation: more devoted to the service of humanity, more committed to the solving of social problems. To what is this change due?*

There's no doubt about it: there have been changes in the Society and there will be more. We remain faithful however to the inspiration of Ignatius, and this is why the Society's devotion to the Church, our efforts to respond to needs indicated by the Vicar of Christ on earth remain intact and strong. It is this very devotion, this very effort to respond to the Church's demands indicated by the Holy Father, which has transformed the Society in recent times. Our commitment to translating the documents of Vatican II into practice has shaken the Society to its very roots, just as faithfulness to the Council of Trent profoundly modified the Society very shortly after it was founded. Another reason for the change in the Society of Jesus is its traditional presence in the midst of the world: the rapid transformations taking place in history have entailed profound changes in our Order too. To take one example, in the educational sector you can easily imagine how much our institutions have been affected by measures taken by governments, by social demands made by trade unions, by financial burdens, by new methods of teaching and management. At a deeper level there has been a cultural revolution with its new language and its new ways of expressing values, which seem to make communication impossible between one generation and another.

Have the changes suggested to you by the Pope and by your loyalty to history been calmly accepted by all the Jesuits? Aren't there some who find it hard to reconcile these changes with being faithful to Ignatius?

A period of rapid changes can never be a calm time. Our efforts to put the Second Vatican Council into practice and respond to a world in flux haven't always been successful; Jesuits, like so many other members of the Church and human society, have made mistakes and on occasion failed. I would however make the point that our orientation is sound, that we are making every effort we can to respond as Saint Ignatius would have wished his sons to respond in the world of today by serving the Lord's Church.

Religious indifference and atheism

Among the front-line apostolates entrusted to you by the Pope, one is to counter atheism. But isn't religious indifference more widespread and spiritually more dangerous?

Atheism, unbelief, erroneous belief are none of them concepts easily allowing themselves to be confined within walled enclosures or demarcated territories. The frontiers between belief and faith, between religious indifference and life in the Spirit, between practical atheism and witness to the living God, are secretly open ones. This said however, one can't deny that it may well be easier to hold a conversation with a convinced atheist than with someone who believes in some vague force, with someone who adheres to an empty theism such as many people take refuge in today. People think, by this means, to avoid an historical salvation, that salvation embodied in Christ, the historical Jesus, at the same time maintaining that they can do without the Church yet forgetting or not knowing that even from an historical point of view Christianity has been humanity's most important spiritual phenomenon. Now, these tendencies find a certain resonance deep down within every one of us, since there is a force within us that doesn't acknowledge God, that rejects him out of hand. So it isn't odd that indifference and the evil of God's absence should leave us naked, should throw doubt on our holiest deeds and words, and that our apostolic work should, as it were, be submerged in the dark night of faith. This is the experience of not a few people, Jesuits among them, in Western Europe.

Have you a strategy for dealing with this "dark night of faith"?

No, what we have is a spirituality: that based on the paschal mystery, in which God manifests his true presence in weakness, the fruitful weakness of the grain of wheat that disappears in the soil of humanity.

Isn't this mystical talk to conceal your resignation?

Taking, from contemplation of the Lord's Passion, the strength to oppose indifference and atheism certainly isn't giving way to a spirit of defeatism or resignation and lapsing into discouragement. On the contrary, exactly as happens in the paschal mystery, it's looking reality in the face, the whole reality of God and human nature, here and now. In 1985, the Extraordinary Synod of Bishops reaffirmed the meaning of the theology of the cross, without which, as experience shows, the optimism and openness of *Gaudium et spes* would be unrealistic and have little of the paschal strength of the Risen Lord. Instead of remaining paralyzed by a seemingly godless world, we seek his presence in everything that is being created and built for the Kingdom and we actively recognize his presence in all who suffer injustice and destitution and the violence of hatred and persecution.

This is very interesting, but what about proclaiming Christ in the secularized world of today? In what terms do you announce the paschal mystery nowadays?

We're aware our religious language sounds mythological to the scientific and pragmatic mentality of our day. We're aware that Christianity is a later arrival in human history and that it only affects a minority. We are likewise aware that our faith in the person of Jesus Christ involves a disturbing element of chance, which is a feature of the whole history of the Church up to today. And yet we cannot not be faithful to that "We cannot stop proclaiming what we have seen and heard" (Acts 4:20), which has characterized the Church from the time of the Apostles to our own.

Only that the message of the Apostles was so paradoxical but new, and able to disturb by its very novelty. Today, and I'm talking mainly about countries which have an ancient Christian tradition, it's a message we've all heard before and which seems to have lost its cutting edge. I insist: isn't there the need for a new language in which to convey the faith?

Often we adopt a passive stance, waiting for a new language for the faith, a new type of evangelism, the image of a vigorous, perfect Church and all the other means that we might use to go and convert the non-believers. At the Areopagus in Athens, Saint Paul tried the "soft" approach but at Corinth he proclaimed that his evangelistic mission would be condemned to passivity if he didn't dare to be weak with God's weakness, if he didn't dare to preach Christ crucified — which will always be scandal and folly. The Pauline experience is valid for us too: if we don't dare to stammer out the paschal mystery in words which are certainly inadequate and distorting, the new language for the faith that the world so much needs will never come into existence. If we don't have the courage to go out to the encounter, person to person, in situations of inevitable weakness, the new evangelization the Churches of the Western world are calling for will never come about. If we waver over openly showing our solidarity with the Church that brings salvation incarnate in all its human contingency, with all the weakness the gift of God entails, we could perhaps lead people to an elegant, enlightened agnosticism but we shouldn't be preaching Jesus Christ, crucified and risen.

The Society of Jesus in Eastern Europe

Among the front-line apostolates entrusted to the Jesuits by the Pope, there is one directed to the peoples who for years have lived under officially atheistic Marxist regimes. What has it been like for Jesuits in actually socialist countries?

The same as for the Church in general, and it's well known that ever since the war the Church in these countries has been exposed to the most rigorous pressures. Marxist governments have been rabid in their efforts either to destroy it or to transform it into an instrument of their oppressive policies. The capacity for resistance has been greater and more consistent in a country wholly or in large degree Catholic like Poland, where the Church has remained strong and has thus exerted a decisive authority and influence on society. Where, in contrast, a State was polarized between different Christian confessions, as in Rumania, and the Church was the expression of a past less clearly identifiable with the people themselves, there Marxist-Leninist forces did succeed in destroying various Church structures. In this context, communist governments commonly tended to suppress the activities and very existence of religious Orders.

In Rumania and Czechoslovakia all religious Orders, hence the Society too, were dispersed, not by a formal law but by an administrative decision of the Ministry of the Interior. The Society was also dispersed in Hungary, where not all Orders were expelled. In Yugoslavia attempts were made to hinder or actually disperse some religious Orders but not on any serious scale. In Poland, the proposal to close the churches and religious houses failed, thanks to the determined resistance of Cardinal Wyszynski and the entire episcopate. In East Germany the activities of the religious Orders were strictly curtailed. It only remains to mention Albania, which was proclaimed an atheist state and where the situation is still tragic: all religious activities are forbidden and are often punished with extraordinary severity.

The survey you have just given is changing rapidly under the impetus of Gorbachev's restructuring or perestroika. Is the new situation a temporary one or is it going to last?

In my judgment, the changes that have taken and are taking place in the countries formerly defined as satellites of the Soviet Union are irreversible, even though traces of the recent past will certainly linger on. In most of these countries, the tendency to abandon Marxist socialism is very clear. The case of the Soviet Union is different, for there Gorbachev talks of restructuring, not of putting an end to the Marxist-Leninist system.

Won't the great transformations taking place in Central and Eastern Europe cause or suggest changes in non-European communist systems such as the Chinese?

The rulers of non-European communist countries insist that the history of their respective revolutions is quite different from that of European communist states. In effect, communism was more or less imposed on the nations of Central and Eastern Europe by the Red Army and interrupted experiments in democracy which they are now painfully trying to resume. In the non-European countries, by way of contrast, communism came to power by overthrowing dictatorial regimes or at least in situations where democracy had never been tried. That is to say, a democratic alternative to the present totalitarian regimes is lacking in these peoples' history.

Might not a democratic alternative be foreseeable, due precisely to changes in the communist bloc?

It's hard to tell. For the moment, the changes in the Soviet Union and the other countries of Central and Eastern Europe seem to be having the effect of making the non-European countries shut themselves off. One just wonders how long they can be content with a merely negative defence, with shutting themselves off from the very developments of Marxism itself.

Let's turn to Eastern Europe and the task of Christians there. What contribution can the Church make towards rebuilding society in Central and Eastern Europe?

The Church has moral authority for a considerable part of the population in these countries. It's significant that respect for the Church's moral authority has recently become apparent in Bohemia, Slovakia, Lithuania, Poland, Croatia and Slovenia; it's a respect shown by non-believers too. In recent years there has been recognition of the Church's role in giving moral support to society's aspirations for a freer, more democratic way of life and one more consistent with human dignity. This recognition can strengthen the Church's influence on the rebuilding of society in Central and Eastern Europe. But, because in past decades the Church has been excluded from the political and social sphere, it

now needs to prepare itself before undertaking activities and
initiatives in the social and cultural field. The Church is expected
to contribute towards stopping the progressive ethico-psycho-
logical degradation of peoples and the progressive disintegration
of social and inter-personal relations. With the great moral authority it enjoys among the people, the Church will be able to
develop a fundamental role in restoring confidence and healthy
attitudes.

*In the new conditions in Central and Eastern Europe, how
will relations between Catholics (of Latin and Oriental rites) and
Orthodox evolve?*

This is a very delicate matter, involving the recognition of
the rights of the Oriental Churches which are in union with Rome.
Restoring these rights will test the excellent ecumenical relations
already existing in some countries, like Russia and Rumania.

*Won't the opening up of these countries to the activities of the
Catholic Church raise fears in the Orthodox Churches that their
Christian communities are going to be latinized?*

I don't think there's any reason for alarm on that score. The
Eastern Church is, generally speaking, deeply rooted in the
hearts of the people, and the danger of latinization doesn't exist.
The problem lies, rather, within the Eastern tradition and arises
from the endless dilemma between closer union with Rome or a
strengthening of the Orthodox community. As far as that goes,
the entire Orthodox world — not merely that of Eastern Europe
— has always feared an invasive Roman Catholic Church because
of its great number of faithful and its many types of social activity.
Fear isn't therefore of being latinized so much as of losing a
tradition, an ecclesiology, a culture. Good ecumenical relations
however should overcome even these sorts of fear.

I suppose the Society of Jesus is drawing up new plans for a pastoral presence in Central and Eastern Europe. In which sectors?

In the Provinces of that part of Europe, the Jesuits have begun to realize how urgently action is needed to cope adequately with the new situation. There is an increasingly obvious need for us to take a serious look at the profile of our own works and play a committed part in the process of drawing up adequate overall plans for the apostolate. The Society is trying to help the Church in a way consistent with its own special talents, by offering to contribute to a more thorough training of the clergy, and to the widening of contacts with the outside world, beyond the Church frontiers. This latter commitment involves a greater Jesuit presence in those circles where decisions are taken affecting the orientation of social life and the propagation of cultural values. There is ever more evidence of the need for a renewal of faith, which hitherto had to be and was a private matter, banished from the public sphere; and at the same time, a great need emerges for training the laity to be the carriers of Christian values in the family and in social, cultural and professional environments. Of great importance too is the apostolate through professional associations (teachers, workers, writers, engineers etc.), which has been strictly forbidden over the past forty years. In a society now become pluralist, the Church has to seek its own position by means of lay people able to shoulder responsibility in these new conditions. Because of this, we are thinking of reorganizing a number of pastoral centers for training Christians in the social, cultural and economic fields. The Society's commitment will also be growing in the field of publications and the mass media. It goes without saying that, very soon, contacts with the world of culture and science, generally speaking very secularized and alienated from the Church, are likely to pose a challenge for the Society to seek new forms of intellectual apostolate.

In non-European socialist countries is there any lifting of the restrictions on religious liberty? You spoke of Vietnam a little while ago; would you care to give your opinion on the situation of the Church in Cuba?

Yes: in Cuba there is freedom for pastoral activity. Also, in recent days, the Government has allowed a fair number of priests and of religious of both sexes into the country, and Jesuits too. This makes it possible for the Church to widen its sphere of action, in response to the growing religious demand of many Cubans, especially the young.

In talking of countries with communist governments, we can't ignore the People's Republic of China, especially since the Pope, when addressing the Gregorian on the occasion of the fourth centenary of Father Matteo Ricci's arrival in China, expressly asked you to take part in the evangelization of the Chinese nation. How are you going to respond to the Pontiff's hopes?

The Society of Jesus was the first, of all the religious Orders which have worked in continental China, to renew its interest in this country and set up a permanent structure. This happened in 1974 at the request of Pope Paul VI. We are continuing this work, adapting it to the developing situation. As far as I can tell, the Society has more personnel invested in this undertaking than all other religious institutes put together.

The difficulties of dialogue with Islam

Let's go on to another front-line apostolate entrusted to you by the Pope: dialogue with non-Christian religions. You've lived for twenty-five years in Lebanon, you've had contact with Moslem believers. Have you ever tried to hold a dialogue with the followers of Islam? More important still, is religious dialogue possible with Moslems?

Dialogue is possible, but clarity's the thing. Dialogues begun by putting confidence in similarities accepted without much discernment can only lead to sentimental and superficial agreements. If the dialogue is conducted without sincerity, there can be no true meeting of minds between those taking part. Manipulating Islam to make it a mirror-image of Christianity impedes true contact and dialogue in depth with living, present-day Islam. Moslems and Christians proclaim themselves to be children of Abraham, yet we are not in fact brothers in Abraham, but in Christ. For Islam, Abraham is the first monotheist, while for Christians he is the father of the covenant between God and his people: an inconceivable thing for a Moslem. Similarly, the Virgin Mary is venerated by Catholic believers and by Moslems. Yet for Moslems she is only the miracle of God's omnipotence: God can do anything, so why shouldn't he be able to turn motherhood into virginity? Whereas for Christians, Mary is the new creature who, through her free assent, was forechosen to be the Theotokos, the Mother of God. Thus Mary becomes the icon of the Church, offering an ideal of consecrated virginity which is unthinkable in Islam. To refuse, because of a false sense of charity, to face up to Islam, with all the apparent, insuperable difficulties that acceptance of the truth entails, means taking the risk of depriving Moslems of the path to a true understanding of Christianity.

We hear a lot about Islamic fundamentalism today, and religious and political agitation in the Arab world is attributed to it. Should we look on this fundamentalism as a passing phenomenon?

The intolerant and aggressive character of *jihad* has its source in a theological concept of the will of God. Islam is faith in God and in his Book. The Koran is not merely central to Islam; it is its essence. For Christians, the Incarnate Word is the immediate Word of God, while the Bible is the mediated Word. For Moslems, in contrast, the Koran as book is the immediate Word of God. Christians wish the Bible to be translated into every language and spread throughout the world; Islam finds it hard to accept that the Koran, having been revealed in Arabic by God, can be prayed, read and written in any language other than the one in which God himself revealed it. Now, the Koran, the essence of Islam, is a law. Hence the ordinances found in it are divine and, since the explicit will of God, are universally binding on everyone, everywhere. They are definitive, having binding force to the end of time. To take one example: the Ramadan fast hasn't altered in the course of many hundreds of years. The notion of renewal, of adaptation or revision, which in Christianity are the fruit of the Spirit, conflicts with the divine character of every ordinance of Islam.

These points having been made, let me now give you an answer to your question. What we call Islamic fundamentalism is not a passing phenomenon, nor is it the expression of some individual's fanaticism: it is Islam as it's supposed to be. Hence the difficulty, for a Middle Eastern government, of opposing the will of God. Christians deeply believe that the Spirit guides the Church, by means of renewal, towards the whole, entire truth of God. Islam has to follow an immutable datum, since that has been divinely revealed; hence its intolerant, fanatical and fundamentalist aspect, summed up in the unfortunate expression, "holy war." It's clear I'm referring to the Islamic religion as such; I'm not passing judgment on the individual Moslem, nor on his faith in God, nor on his faithfulness to the Koran.

The problems you've mentioned notwithstanding, the Catholic Church has opened a dialogue with Islam. What fruits may we hope for?

In the Conciliar declaration *Nostra aetate,* the Church invited Catholics to nourish respect and esteem for Moslems. While recognizing the conflicts and misunderstandings that have often marked relations between Christians and Moslems in the past, the Council Fathers encouraged Christians and Moslems to collaborate with a view to spreading peace, social justice, moral values and human freedom throughout the world. This common charge to those who believe in God was renewed by Popes Paul VI and John Paul II. Faith in God, common to Christians and Moslems, together with their elder brother, the Jewish people, as descendants of Abraham in faith, ought to be the basis for a common witness of faith. In addressing young Moslems in Morocco, John Paul II declared that we should bear witness to the spiritual values of which the world stands in need, and the first of these is faith in God. In the *Formula* of the Society of Jesus, it says that the Jesuit is sent to the Turks, not as to enemies however, nor in a crusading spirit, but rather by going among them with friendliness and love. We are sent in imitation of Ignatius, who went to Palestine as a man of faith, humble and sincere, anxious only to serve others in what concerns the spiritual life, not with warlike discipline but as a worker of peace. We are taking part in this dialogue between Catholics and Moslems precisely in that sort of spirit, by listening and learning and also by bearing witness and offering. As to the fruits, if God wills, he will make them ripen by what means and in what times he pleases.

Let's take a concrete example. In Lebanon, where you lived for more than twenty-five years, is it possible for Christians and Moslems to live at peace together?

The problem is a very complex one. First of all, there's the question about recognizing the independence of Lebanon, and this doesn't depend on the Lebanese. As a consequence of the state of war, provoked by the struggle for the right of the Palestinians to have a homeland, foreign forces have thought fit to occupy large areas of Lebanon. Only an international conference could sort this problem out, restore peace in the Middle East and re-establish Lebanese independence. Then there's the problem directly concerning the Lebanese themselves. Lebanon, inhabited by communities with widely differing interests, cultures and mentalities, hasn't had the time it needs to become a true nation. To defend themselves, these communities have all too often resorted to violence and almost always with the help and complicity of non-Lebanese forces. The various communities are now however beginning to grasp the fact that they are condemned to work together if they do not wish to perish; they will have to hammer out a new political formula together, which will allow them all to live in harmony. These problems are influenced but not entirely dominated by the strong tension, if not the actual incompatibility, which seemingly exists between the Moslem world and Christendom, to both of which worlds the Lebanese belong. Being the only country in the Middle East where Islam doesn't have an overwhelming majority, Lebanon has dreams of being a model of co-existence, dialogue and tolerance.

Without managing to be one. — Doesn't the real obstacle lie in the basic intolerance of Islam?

Despite the dominant role of Moslem fanaticism in a complex situation, Christians and Moslems are too much believers not to condemn acts of inhuman violence, acts that can't be justified in God's name and that distort the true face of Islam and Christianity. In this context, the coherent witness of those Christians who are in contact with the Middle East for reasons of diplomacy, trade, relief work or cultural tourism, is important. Be it said however that Christians visiting the Middle East, that land of believers, don't always present a positive image of their faith.

Ecumenical dialogue is not marking time

Another of your front-line activities is ecumenical dialogue. What contribution is the Society making to the quest for Christian unity?

I have lived my priestly life in the Eastern Church, in the Armenian Church to be precise. Other Superiors General, and in particular Father Ledochowski, have been sympathetic to the presence, in the Society, of Jesuits belonging to the Eastern Churches and aware of the help the Society could give these Churches. For myself, the training I received has sensitized me to ecumenism, to the Lord's will that there should be full communion between all Christian Churches. We must not resign ourselves to being divided. We ought to be aware that the disunity of Christians is a real scandal preventing the spread of the Gospel of love.

Aren't there a few points on which the Society might reproach itself with regard to its historical relations with the Eastern Churches?

Well, yes, relations between the Eastern Churches and the Society have had their difficult and sometimes painful moments in the past. In defence of the ministry of Peter, the Latin missionaries, and hence the Jesuits too, didn't always recognize the genuinely Christian content of the Eastern traditions. If the Jesuits strongly supported those Eastern Churches which were in union with Rome, it was mainly to stress that it was perfectly possible to be true Eastern Christians while remaining in perfect communion with the Holy See. Even today the Churches confront one another over this problem, which rather than encourage unity seems to obstruct it, since it is misunderstood.

What contribution are the Jesuits making today towards improving relations between Catholics and the Orthodox?

By means of our educational institutions in Europe and the Middle East, and with our specialized centers like the Pontifical Oriental Institute and the Pontifical Russian College — only to mention the two most important ones in Rome — we Jesuits

maintain research and study relations with the Eastern
Churches, both Catholic and Orthodox, in the hope of fostering
full communion between the sister Churches, to use the expression of Paul VI and John Paul II.

*Do you think, as many people in the Catholic Church and other
Churches think, that ecumenical dialogue is now marking time, in
contrast to the enthusiasm and the initiatives sparked off by Vatican
II?*

Some people do indeed think that the obstacles are greater
today than they were twenty-five years ago. The fact is that
before the Second Vatican Council problems barely existed, for
the simple reason that the Churches didn't have reciprocal relations. Today's problems arise from two causes. First, because, in
the ecumenical dialogue, we have got nearer and nearer to the
core of the doctrinal disagreements that largely differentiate one
Church from another. The second cause lies in the breadth of the
discussions: today when a problem arises in the course of dialogue, it is debated in ever-widening circles by pastors, theologians
and the faithful, slowing everything down yet making for deeper
understanding on a truly common journey.

On the other hand, there are many signs of a will to continue
the common quest for unity and collaboration. The meeting at
Basel in May 1989 gave very clear indication of this. And it's also
worth remembering that, during the apostolic journeys of the
Holy Father, significant and intense moments of ecumenical
dialogue are constantly taking place. Hence I would say there's no
need to feel discouraged, even if we don't see Christian unity just
round the corner. Dom Couturier, one of the great apostles of
ecumenism, loved to say that Church unity is the Lord's work and
only the Lord knows how and when it will come about. Certainly
we ought to work together, for the divisions in Christendom are, I
repeat, a scandal, and we can't ask the world to make peace while
we give proof of not being able to live at peace among ourselves,

notwithstanding the fact that we are brothers and sisters in Christ.

This is the point: a lot of people think that today the will to overcome the obstacles dividing Christians is weaker than it was.

I don't think so. I also believe that the will is more realistic now than twenty-five years ago, because now we know more about what the obstacles are that separate us from one another and, notwithstanding that, dialogue goes on. Besides, ecumenism is no longer a matter of enthusiasm, emotions or formalistic sessions among experts; it is a fact permeating the very life of the whole Church.

Doesn't it strike you that even today ecumenical dialogue is largely an affair of bilateral or multi-lateral meetings of theologians and other experts, while the people of God remain fairly indifferent?

No, I think the people of God are playing their part with a very clear desire for unity. I have experienced this personally at ecumenical gatherings between Catholics and Orthodox in Crete and at Bari. Someone actually shouted out in the street, in very heated language: "You theologians and experts will be the ones to blame if the Church goes on being divided; the people of God want to live in harmony with all Christians." From this admittedly rather naive protest you can see the desire for unity that inspired it; at the same time it must be pointed out that, just as it is acceptable that people should live together for superficial reasons, so it should be acceptable that they should remain divided for profound ones. And centuries of antagonism and failure to communicate have deepened the chasm of separation. Lastly, one can't approach ecumenism in the expectation of "a happy ending," for the way to unity has as its goal unity under the Cross of Christ, and this tells us straightaway that progress isn't likely to be easy. Slowly but surely, however, dialogue advances.

You are a member of the Catholic Commission for Dialogue with the Orthodox. How far have you gotten with your work?

We're getting on well, I should say. Today we have reached the point of asking ourselves this question, which represents the perspective in which we shall be working in the future: It is clear that there are still differences between us, but are they such as to prevent us from entering full communion? We're not concerned about eliminating the differences but about finding out whether they are so grave as to rule out unity. Like other observers, I too think that the things we have in common, which unite us to the Orthodox, far outweigh those things that historically have divided us for centuries.

8

THE CHALLENGES
OF THE MODERN WORLD

Secularization and its ambiguities

Cultural pluralism, religious indifference, widespread economic well-being, great faith in science and technology: these are the dominant characteristics of the modern world and constitute a range of challenges for the Church and, within it, the Society of Jesus. How is the modern world to be converted?

The Church's response to these challenges can only be what it has always been: the Gospel. The Society, and religious life in general, logically proceeds in the same direction. With the commitment to live the evangelical counsels of chastity, poverty and obedience, the members of religious Orders tell present-day society that it's possible to live by values other than those of an exasperated consumerism and of total personal independence. The eschatological response is what in essence distinguishes all religious life: monks respond with contemplation and the solitude of the cloister; religious of apostolic life, with their involvement in the world; but one and other mean to remind society that material progress isn't everything, that there can't be a New Earth without Heaven. The religious remind society that God is not against well-being but that this well-being doesn't satisfy the whole of human nature, since human beings don't live by bread alone.

119

They acknowledge that God has given human beings intelligence and reason in order to make progress in science, but remind the world that the human heart can never be satisfied with the finite achievements of science, it having been made for the infinite. Religious indeed, by the gratuitous gift of self which characterizes their life, summon society not to regard rigorous technological effectiveness as an absolute. In other words, the Church and within it religious life, seeks to build a commonwealth, which lies within God's plans; and we know that God's designs are not those of human beings, for whom there can only be tension and challenge between world and Church. It seems to me that a deep awareness of this radical dialectic would be the most appropriate attitude for a pastoral response to the challenges of modern society.

Religious publicists constantly assert that secularization is spreading in the modern world, and the term is always used in a negative sense. But hasn't secularization also got positive connotations, if we understand it as the proper autonomy of terrestrial things from the religious sphere?

It seems to me that the whole Bible prompts human beings to exercise responsibility. Its message is that to the call of God a filial, not a servile, response must be given. Jesus, who is the model of the new human creature, throughout his life gives a free response to the Father's will. In this I find the basis for all true autonomy of terrestrial things, for secularization, as is explained in the Conciliar Constitution *Gaudium et spes*. On this point it is rewarding to contrast the Bible with the Koran. In the Koran, God creates Adam and the animals, then gives the animals names, which Adam repeats; in the Bible, as you know, it is Adam who names the animals. This, symbolically stated, is the recognition of human autonomy in relation to terrestrial things. If to the term secularization you give this sense of autonomous responsibility towards creation, this is positive; it becomes negative when the autonomy of terrestrial things is not seen for what it truly is, that is to say, when we forget that God is the source and end of all creation. We must, in a word, distinguish between human autonomy and human self-sufficiency: in the first case we mean free responsibility before God; in the second, the human creature divorces himself from his Creator.

The phenomenon of secularization, understood in the negative sense, seems mainly to distinguish those societies which have been Christian longest? Why?

In origin and substance, Christianity isn't a system, isn't an ideology; it's the free response of human beings to Christ. But little by little it has become a system, with values conditioned by the customs and institutions of the countries of most long-standing Christian tradition. At a given moment in historical evolution, these values are lived as though they didn't have their source in Christ and are now perceived as sufficient in themselves; but in the process they lose their true efficacy, they lose their positive strength for humanity.

Human values are not sufficient in themselves

Don't you think the acceptance of Christian values demonstrates the historical effectiveness of Christianity, even though the source of those values has been forgotten?

I doubt it very much. Suppose we had to make an act of self-sacrifice to live by those values, for whose sake would we make it? People, being sinners, can't live these values by their own efforts; they need grace, that is to say, life in Christ.

But it's a fact that many Christian values are accepted and lived today without conscious reference to the Gospel.

I'm not denying that this happens. What I'm saying is that our heart isn't keen on dying to self: on the contrary, it seeks its own interest. One may even insist on those values while denying the existence of sin (and of grace), but at the moment of crisis, of a conflict of interests, for the sake of what would one make the act of renunciation? Without direct or even tacit reference to the Absolute, what meaning have life and death, pain and love? To give meaning to our present and future existence, there has to be surrender to Christ and the help of his might.

It can't however be denied that in many secular states the values of freedom, justice, honesty, respect for others — which we are accustomed to think of as being rooted in Christianity — are lived by the great majority of citizens without any reference to Christ. Doesn't this prove that a secular humanism can exist quite independently of any religious basis?

The Church deeply believes that the Spirit of the Lord fills the universe, and doesn't find it strange that the might of the Spirit should sustain all that is true, free, just. At the same time, the Church knows that human beings are weak and that, without recognizing the might of the Spirit of Christ, human truth, human freedom, human justice are always in danger of being perverted or misdirected.

Some writers hold that the process of secularization has furthermore been injected with a form of protest against the excessive power of the Church, which in times past and particularly in societies where it was strongest, interfered directly in many fields which did not fall within its competence. Do you agree?

Perhaps to put it like this is to state a complex problem in over-simple terms. Of course, in certain cases, there have been deviations of this sort. But normally the Church has spoken and speaks to remind the world that human values are not self-sufficient but relative to God. And we shouldn't forget that the Church often intervenes to safeguard the autonomy of those values, that is to say, their intrinsic nature. For instance, when the Church teaches that human life ought never to be suppressed, not even in its embryonic form, it isn't doing this to impose limitations on scientific progress, but to prevent such progress as might rebound on the human race. Another example is John Paul II's teaching on labor. Economic theory would have it that unemployment is the accidental product of a market economy and that the Christian faith has nothing relevant to say about it. People don't understand or pretend they don't understand that when the Church intervenes in this domain it isn't putting forward some new economic theory, but simply maintaining, to safeguard people, who have the right to work, that it is unacceptable for unemployment to be regarded as an accident, as the price that has to be paid for a market economy to function. Here, the Church is not only respecting the economy but safeguarding it as a value; for, if the economy destroys its human work-force, it can no longer be considered to have value for us.

In the modern world there seems to be a schizophrenic attitude towards advances in the scientific and technological fields. On the one hand, these are appreciated for the great advantages they confer on the human race; on the other, they are blamed for being at the root of many disasters (not least the manipulation of human genetics). What should a Christian's attitude be toward science and technology?

I premise that a Christian should have the defense of humanity as his first concern, since God wills that human beings should live; whereas science and technology are often in danger of moving according to a dynamism unrelated to the genuine service of the human race. So it's our job to keep recalling science and technology to their true purpose as instruments to serve the human race. Let me remind you of John Paul II's teaching in the encyclical *Sollicitudo rei socialis* that an economy that pushes so many people to the margins of society cannot be regarded as serving human progress. Again, in this case, the Church isn't against but rather in favor of a genuinely human progress.

The Society has a great many men and institutions active in the cultural sphere; what is it doing to encourage a balanced employment of science and technology?

In the past there was a tendency to think that only people teaching philosophy, theology or the humanities were conveying values. Today, throughout the Society, we insist on the fact that all teaching conveys values and that teachers, in their respective fields, must not ignore the entirety of human society, viewed in accordance with God's plan. Consequently we recognize the value of science and technology, while at the same time we give them their true place in the relationship between God and human beings. All our activities in the cultural field must share in that integrated vision.

Ecological and pacifist movements

In the more advanced societies, awareness of and commitment to the environment is now growing, especially among the young. What part can the Church play in this movement, given that it is both ethical and political?

The Church has a great tradition in this regard, and it's expressed particularly in Franciscan spirituality. It's no accident that the city of Assisi has become an important landmark for anyone who's committed to peace and ecology. The Church's role in the ecological movement is that of sustaining ethical awareness about the urgency of safeguarding the created world for present and future generations. But I should like to make the point too that Ignatian spirituality isn't in fact alien to an ecological view (rightly understood) of the world and the use of the creatures in it. We should re-read and ponder deeply on Ignatius's important reflection "on obtaining love" in this perspective. At the end of the *Spiritual Exercises,* he joins us in discovering "how all good things and all gifts descend from above," from the God of light. How are these gifts to be used, lavished as they are on us by God, the Creator of the cosmos and of us? The answer, so topical today, is already specified in the *First Principle and Foundation* of the same *Spiritual Exercises.* It is the famous Ignatian spiritual criterion of the *tantum, quantum*: "Man must make use of them (all things in the universe) insofar as they help him to attain his end, and in the same way he ought to withdraw from them insofar as they hinder him from it."

You know that one wing of the ecological movement accuses the Judaeo-Christian tradition of being responsible for abuses of nature, by virtue of the biblical command: "Grow, multiply, dominate the earth." Are there any grounds for this?

No, the accusation is without foundation since the Bible itself teaches that God has entrusted the natural world to the care and responsibility of the human race; the latter however has abused it from the start. Biblical tradition itself accuses the human race of not using the natural world as God wished, that is to say, wisely and lovingly. According to God's original plan, human beings were to have been like shepherds or like gardeners of the created world. No gardener plants all kinds of colorful flowers and trees, only to pull them up and destroy them. This is what human beings do with their perverse use of created things. But the blame lies with human beings, not with God. In the Gospel, further more, we see the Lord treat the natural world with the greatest care and respect. In biblical tradition I see not only how irresponsible use of the earth began, but the best of foundations for a Christian ecology. And on this foundation, a theology of ecology is being worked out today.

Another movement which is fairly widespread in the more advanced countries is pacifism. Is the Society of Jesus doing anything to support this aspiration?

Peace problems have long had a place in the programs of our universities and Social Centers. But the theme of peace can't be the speciality of a handful of scholars or of a few committed people in the social field, any more than it can be generated solely by politicians or those who negotiate disarmament treaties. The peace of the world is everyone's responsibility. Insofar as this concerns the Society as a whole, I think that Jesuits today are very much aware that in the way people speak and act in daily life there are all sorts of occasions that can cause violence to break out. My own experience in the Middle East tells me that a war isn't ever caused merely by the enmity between two or more leaders: there's a whole history beginning within families, in people's homes, where such rancors and dissensions are nurtured as eventually to eliminate all understanding of other people's differences, and thus the fuel is prepared for a violent conflagration.

What specific contributions can the Society of Jesus make towards spreading pacific attitudes of mind?

In our periodicals, Social Centers and universities, we frequently work out detailed analyses of themes connected with peace. One of these, which people perhaps don't talk about very much, is how to stop wars once they have started. All too often we talk about peace in general terms without remembering that wars are actually going on, frequently fueled by the armaments industry which has an interest in keeping the hot-spots burning. We should unmask these interests, if we do not wish to be accomplices, however indirect, of war situations. The point is, essentially, and the Society is well aware of this, to convince ourselves that everything we do or do not do can contribute to the advance or cessation of violence in the world. A handful of leaders is not solely responsible; they need a certain climate, the support of public opinion, before they can act, whether for war or peace.

Don't you think the desire for a less polluted environment and for a world free of the nuclear threat and the arms race, may hide an unconscious selfishness in more advanced societies, unless they insist on these advantages being shared by the developing peoples too?

Yes, I suppose so, and we find ourselves faced with a very clear case here on how values, good in themselves, can be relative and, in the end become non-values if they don't open up to wider perspectives. This is why the Church keeps reminding us that we can't be saved on our own and that, all the while there is war in many parts of the world, the so-called First World can't allow itself to think that everything's OK. The same goes for world hunger: all the while there's famine in Ethiopia and other African and Asian countries, the First World can't settle back and believe as a consequence that the world economy is expanding simply because its own economy is improving. The Church, being universal and hence not confined to this or that country, or to this or that culture, ends up by being the conscience of all humanity. The Pope's travels, to my mind, make this a palpable fact. And again, owing to the constant bombardment of news from radio and TV, there is a growing awareness in the world of all belonging to all, an awareness of the global village.

"Global village" and public opinion

Isn't the real danger that of becoming universal spectators? I mean, doesn't it seem to you that awareness of so many enormous

problems finally paralyzes our individual commitment, since such
great needs make us feel so helpless?

The risk exists, but it can be combated by educating people
to commit themselves, and here again the Church's role is indispensable. I think however that we haven't reached the point of
being blasé about the great dramas of the world. In recent years
there was a great mobilization of concern over the famine in
Ethiopia. More recently still, there was universal condemnation
of the way the young Chinese were treated, who protested in
Tienanmen Square.

Has the universal condemnation of the Chinese authorities
been any use?

Not apparently. But you would have to take the long-term
view, and China has a history going back thousands of years.
After what has happened, the rulers in Peking certainly can't
ignore the reaction of the rest of the world, if only because the
economic development of China depends to a large extent on the
good will, as well as on the interests, of other countries.

Don't you agree that public opinion can be manipulated by
those who control the major means of communication? And isn't the
Third World a certain loser in this field, given that it has neither
large press agencies nor extensive television networks of its own?

Facts are facts and it's hard to manipulate them. It's true that
events are always presented in a context, and this can be colored
by the views of the presenter. But more serious than this sort of
manipulation seems to me to be the selecting of facts by often not
mentioning important events and problems concerning countries
or peoples who don't have sufficient resources to make
themselves heard. Among many other cases, I should like to
mention that of the Kurds, who find it hard to gain access to the
means of communication. Likewise the situation in Lebanon went
unknown to world opinion for a considerable time. The Holy

Father's broken-hearted intervention, which took place on August 15, 1989, when he spoke publicly of the genocide of the Lebanese people and named those responsible for this monstrous crime, had the effect of shattering the silence of the mass media and getting international diplomacy into action.

So manipulation does exist. How can we counter it?

I have no specific remedies. I think that people who work in the media, especially if they are Christians, ought to question themselves about the interests and values to which they accord predominance in their work, and also to see that every opportunity is being taken to give a voice to those who normally have none. I know that in the media market it's hard to keep a rule of this sort, but it is one of the demands of the loving option for the poor that Christ himself has taught us.

"Giving Europe a soul"

I should now like to ask you some questions about Europe. You know that, starting in 1993, Western Europe, with the finalizing of the great common market, will be completing one more step towards an even greater unity. What are likely to be the pastoral consequences of this?

As you mention, we already have a common market and Western European unity is still based on the category of having: wealth, market, advantages, interests, defence, competition with Japan and the United States, etc. There's a risk of only building a Europe of merchants, of bankers. And yet I see that there's a vocation for Europe; since, if it's true that Europe exported colonialism, it's equally true that from Europe Christianity has spread across the world. I think that still today Europe can draw on its own cultural and spiritual heritage, and so have a vocation in the world that's not merely confined to material progress. I think furthermore that only from an inspiration of this sort can spring true unity, such as to overcome the present politico-military blocs in our continent and to fill the growing gap between North and South in the world.

Giving Europe a soul is a recurring catchphrase in Church circles. What does it mean?

It means precisely drawing on the European spiritual heritage, in order to go beyond a combined effort based solely on organizing the market. If we think of the many cases of internal conflict within the European nations — take Spain, Belgium, Northern Ireland for instance — we see there's a need for much more than a common market, if we want Europe to respond to its vocation in the world. It's obvious that for this to happen, catchphrases are not enough. What's needed is a cultural plan and to it Christians can and should make a big contribution with long-term pastoral initiatives.

Another catchphrase invokes Europe's Christian roots, to which such Western values are attributed as the freedom and dignity of the individual. To what roots then should non-values such as individualism, political and religious sectarianism (with war as its tragic sequel) and racism be attributed?

Distortions of the European Christian heritage are responsible for these non-values. We must never forget the parable of the grain and the darnel: good and evil are often mixed up together. The history of the Church is full of this mixture. When Constantine granted freedom to the Church, thereby offering it the protection of the State, this was a positive opportunity for Christians to evangelize; at the same time, that process brought about distortions and negative facts, such as a greater worldliness of the Church. Thus the discovery of other people and continents, with the desire to bring them civilization and the faith, was accompanied by colonialism and the other evils you have mentioned. But rediscovering Europe's Christian roots, a task to which John Paul II frequently summons us Christians and all Europeans, means turning back to draw new sap and new inspiration from the tree of life that has made European civilization great: and this tree — let us not forget — is precisely Christianity.

Was it a good thing to go and "discover" other peoples?

Yes, I should say so. The spread of freedom, of the democratic ideal, in other continents derives from contacts with Europeans. We may complain about the drawbacks of democracy but it remains the political system for which many, many people are still struggling today.

What should relations be between Western Europe and the eastern part of the continent?

Such relations as encourage the building of a common home, as they say today, quoting Gorbachev. This means, in a word, no longer accepting Yalta and the tearing apart of the continent that resulted from that treaty. We have so many things in common: the same origin, the same cultural heritage, the same Christian inheritance; ideological and political reasons alone have divided us. We need to recover the reasons for living together, and they cannot fail primarily to be spiritual ones. The Church has been at pains to emphasize this deeper unity by proclaiming as patrons of Europe, along with Benedict, the two brothers Cyril and Methodius, worthy spokesmen for the Slavonic world, which is fully a part of the European heritage. A recent sign of this spiritual unity was the occasion of the millennium of the Russian Church, which was regarded as a festival by all the European Churches.

Restoring the balance between North and South

And what sort of relations should Europe have with the Third World?

Up till now these relations have been influenced by the tensions between East and West, which certainly hasn't been much help to the Third World. Many countries in process of development have aligned themselves with one or other of the two blocs, more from compelling economic or military reasons than from free political choice. Now North-South relations are attracting more attention and the major problem of restoring the balance between the rich countries and the poor ones is more clearly seen. In the encyclical *Sollicitudo rei socialis,* the Pope forcefully pointed out that the rich world is responsible for the poverty of the rest of the world and that it isn't enough for it to give the poor countries what it has left over; it ought to give part of what it regards as necessary, which means a lowering of the standard of living in the rich countries. The development of the peoples of the North still depends on the under-development of the peoples of the South. So it's no longer enough for a few capitalists to have a change of heart; what's needed is the conversion of a capitalist mentality which has permeated the masses as well. Our people need to realize that it isn't sufficient to help the peoples of the Third World with one-time grants, these being inadequate for solving the problem of North-South relations. What's needed is for us to be convinced we have to embrace a certain austerity of lifestyle, if we really want greater international justice.

Isn't this a bit over-idealistic?

No, it's merely telling things as they are, even if it is true that today only the Church dares to speak out so clearly. In Europe not even the left-wing political parties or trade unions have the audacity to propose an economic policy of austerity for the sake of the Third World to their hard-liners. Hence we go on nourishing the illusion that handouts and one-time grants are enough, when these are only palliatives, not solutions.

You say that only the Church speaks out so clearly. This is true of documents issued by the Pope and many of the episcopates. But can it be said to be equally true of daily pastoral practice, of normal preaching in our churches?

Ordinary pastoral work has to reckon with a certain amount of resistance from many Christians on these topics. Since the translation of the Magisterium's directives into practical terms means giving up part of our well-being, even Christians — who aren't all angels — have difficulty in adopting this line of thought. Hence the invitations to the Church, especially from wealthier Christians, to keep its attention on holy things and let other people deal with the Third World, the balance of payments and international justice. And since the Church's pastoral activity needs the economic support of Christians and in particular of the richer ones, you can see why these topics are aired rather cautiously. We need to react however, for the sake of that which has substance in those holy things. At the beginning, the Eucharist was also an expression of the having all things in common among Christians, so that no one suffered in penury. Today that survives in the Offertory, now purely symbolic. We need to recover the substance. And the substance is that the Church can't celebrate the Eucharist without sharing the Savior's gift of life with the poor: and that, materially too; not only spiritually. In other words, we need to recover the sense of *diakonia,* of serving and sharing, which are part of the nature of the Eucharist. This sort of sharing becomes effective solidarity or "social love," as Paul VI called it.

That's another conversion demanded of Christians. But there's no end to the conversions required. An adjustment of mental approach and pastoral method is needed to cope with the very rapid social changes we are witnessing, especially in the Western world. Is the Society "converting" its own works and methods with the agility that social changes demand?

Constant evaluation of what we are doing forms part of the Society's spiritual life. In the *Spiritual Exercises* which, either on our own or communally, we make every year, questions like this constantly recur: What am I doing for Christ? Is what I'm doing really what he is asking of me now? In our Provinces, furthermore, we regularly hold planning sessions which is a form of discernment of needs balanced against resources and works in progress. It may then happen that a work, even if in the past it proved apostolically very worthwhile, gets altered or suppressed, so that we can have more people available for new undertakings. This requires true conversion, since we all have a tendency to become wedded to our work and always to regard as most useful the project in which we ourselves are engaged. However, I must concede that in this respect there's plenty of dynamism in the Society and that in the long-term planning which I have just mentioned there usually emerges a remarkable readiness for the changes that apostolic necessities impose. One instrument, to facilitate our planning in a spirit of sharing of goods and of *diakonia* (service) to the poor, is FACSI, an acronym for the Father General's Charitable Fund. This accepts contributions from the Society's communities throughout the world and distributes them in areas of greatest need, by financing — within the bounds of possibility — social and spiritual projects which have been put forward but which have no other resources. Perhaps this isn't much but we always try to achieve something worthwhile year by year.

Towards the third millennium

John Paul II often refers to the third millennium of Christianity, which will begin in ten years' time. Does the Society have a long-term plan for dealing with the challenges ahead?

The Society is, first and foremost, ready to work for the Holy Father's pastoral plan as regards the third millennium. For my part, I have at least one hope: the first Christian millennium was that of communion among Christians; the second millennium witnessed the great divisions among us; the third, I hope, will be the one of communion regained. I believe the Society will go on working for this and for the new evangelization of which the Pope is constantly talking.

What are we to understand by "new evangelization"?

Proclaiming the Gospel in a language that speaks to the minds and touches the hearts of people today. Here a problem immediately arises: modern idioms are positivist and empirical since conditioned by technology, and the Church cannot use them, for the Church has to speak of the mystery of God, which cannot be expressed in mathematical language. On the other hand, the Church cannot speak to the modern world in an archaic or sermonizing way. I personally believe we are going to discover the idiom for the new evangelization by degrees, as we become involved in the new evangelization itself; and in any case, however we speak about the mystery of God, we shall only be stammering, for this is infinitely richer than all our attempts to put it into words. It would however be wrong to keep quiet, just because we see that on many occasions our idiom is inadequate and unincisive. All the same, I am convinced that the new evangelization does need a new idiom and a dialogue with the world, so that we can grasp in depth what the expectations and problems exactly are; but it will just as much need people who will give their testimony by singing alleluia, that is to say, it will need charismatic figures. Naturally, the new evangelization won't be able to do without the prayers, liturgical celebrations and communal experiences of believers. This last point strikes me as particularly important. I am indeed convinced that the new evangelization won't get anywhere without these groups of Christians bearing joyful, communal witness to their faith: this can be done in movements, parishes or monasteries but the important thing is to repeat the example of that first community in Jerusalem when the Christians were of one heart and soul and no one went in need. Another element of the new evangelization will certainly be commitment to the poor; a Church that doesn't care about those who suffer is not living the Gospel. Fortunately, Christian feeling for the poor is on the increase and so, from this point of view, the new evangelization has already begun.

9

IN THE COMMUNITY OF BELIEVERS

The Jesuits in the local Churches

We have already discussed the relations between the Pope and the Society. I should now like to ask a few questions about the relations between the Jesuits and other Church entities. Let's begin with the bishops who are principally responsible for the life of the local Churches. Do you run into difficulties over coordinating your work with the pastoral plans of local Christian communities?

Yes, we do; and the reason lies in the apostolic purpose of the Society, which can't be circumscribed within the scope of a local Church. This isn't something merely affecting Jesuits. It affects most of the religious Families and many of the new movements in the Church as well. One and other are called by the Spirit and recognized by the Church to perform a precise task or give a particular witness. The problem doesn't exist for monastic religious life, since this plays no direct part in diocesan pastoral plans. It's different however for those religious institutes or ecclesial movements which have a precise apostolic vocation and, at the same time, have to acknowledge that the bishop is the pastor of the local Church. In this case, this religious Family or that movement has to find out how it can play a part in the diocesan pastoral plan, with its own specific contribution. In this respect, it's important to stress that the scope of the diocesan plan should be wide, that is to say, it should not be confined to strictly parochial work, particularly since the said local Church has other commitments, such as health care, culture, etc., and hence the religious Families that care for the sick or the teaching of the young should be able to integrate into the local Church's pastoral plans. At the same time, a diocese might need a particular commitment as regards education, but the religious Families living within its territory might not be called to this particular apostolate. To harmonize all these factors requires a great labor of communication, of really and truly "mutual relations," to quote the title of a well-known document issued by the Holy See. While religious Families try to respond to the pastoral concerns of the Holy See, the bishops for their part ought to see how religious life, which is a gift of the Spirit to the Church, can be integrated into their own pastoral plans.

Don't you think a lot of tension could be avoided if religious were more involved in preparing the pastoral plans of local Churches?

Very probably. It must be stressed however that, while the religious Family has to be faithful to its commitment which it has received as a charism from the Lord, it cannot impose this same charism on a diocese's pastoral plan. It's a different matter, of course, if the charism happens to integrate well with the pastoral plan; then, no doubt, close collaboration can be very fruitful.

Since the Holy See's document Mutual relations *appeared, have relations in fact improved between religious and local Churches?*

In some parts of the world, yes; in others, not so much. For instance, in the United States since the visit to the religious Institutes made by a delegation of bishops on the orders of the Holy See, I think we may say the bishops have a rather better understanding of religious life and its purposes, and this has greatly contributed to a closer contact between the various components of the Church. In other parts of the world, there are local Churches where mutual relations are limited to cordial indifference. Not to mention a certain attitude of aggressiveness to be found in one or two regions, and that very certainly does not correspond to the spirit of communion in the Church.

Aggressiveness on whose part?

Best not to go into that too deeply! Suffice it to remark that in the past, religious enjoyed great autonomy. Today the Church doesn't intend to restrict this autonomy but wants apostolic work done in communion, under the Holy Father and the bishops, to be given special prominence. And this is why everyone ought to collaborate over seeing what specific contributions the various religious Families can make. And this raises difficulties, I tell you.

But don't these difficulties mainly belong to the past?

No, quite the reverse. The difficulties are today's and can get worse if we don't all become persuaded that we can't work on our own. It's our urgent duty, incumbent on us all, to enter into an authentic communion of thought. This doesn't mean suffocating our tensions and conflicts. Tensions and conflicts aren't always exclusively negative things. Sometimes they are the starting point for needful clarifications. For instance, there are many bishops who dare not intervene when they know they should, because they're frightened the religious might leave their dioceses. This is certainly not symptomatic of acting in communion. In other cases, bishops who find themselves short-handed ask religious to take on jobs which haven't the least relationship to their charism, and this can cause difficulties too.

What difficulties, given that the bishop is in overall charge of pastoral activities in the local Church and that it's therefore up to him to indicate which jobs should take priority?

But it's equally true that a religious institute has its own charism to put at the service of the whole Church, a charism that the pastors of local Churches ought not lightly to undervalue. Besides, the religious superior has the right to withdraw his personnel for duties that he may consider more urgent. This is where the tensions can arise, especially in those dioceses where there is such a shortage of clergy that the bishops have to hand many responsibilities over to the religious.

And how do you try to overcome these difficulties?

More and more often nowadays, religious Families have a sort of contract with the bishop, by the terms of which various contingencies are envisaged. Provision is even made for the bishop on occasion to have his say in the appointment or transfer of religious.

Many religious work for National Bishops' Conferences. In your view, do these Bishops' Conferences, which have developed a great deal, especially since Vatican II, have merely an organizational function, or are they an expression of episcopal collegiality with a theological basis?

I don't want to go into the theological problem, which un-doubtedly exists, about the magisterial role or not of Bishops' Conferences. Suffice it to say that there's no doubting the fact that Bishops' Conferences are a fine expression of communion and collaboration within the Church. The criticisms sometimes levelled against Bishops' Conferences aren't concerned with their existence or the role they are regaining in the Church. If any-thing, they're concerned with two dangers: the one is that the bishop may forget that, magisterially and sacramentally, he is fully responsible within his own diocese; the other is the risk all organizations run, where a large number of people are employed, that is to say, proliferating bureaucracy. Then it's easy to understand that the bishops can't manage to express themselves freely and frankly any more, hemmed in as they are by orders of the day, by draft documents drawn up by permanent officials, by in-house minutes and balance-sheets to be approved. This is the price to be paid when work is organized on a collective basis. But it's a price that undoubtedly falls short of the advantages. Furthermore, the Holy See normally turns to Bishops' Conferences for consultation or communication. It does so because this is consistent with the logic of collegiality, restored to value by Vatican II.

"Roman centralism" and the nomination of bishops

Not a few theologians, and some bishops too, have recently denounced the reemergence of the centralism of the Roman Curia at the expense of the local Churches. Is this just futile alarmism?

The Roman Curia operates as the central administration of the Church. Now, to charge it with centralism doesn't make sense; that is precisely its role: to operate out of the center. Furthermore, it seems to me that, since Vatican II, there has been a healthy and productive equilibrium in relations between the Roman Curia and the periphery of the Church, largely due to constant consultation between the Holy See and Bishops' Conferences. That said, it's more than normal that the perspectives of someone working at the center will be different from those of someone working on the periphery.

But perhaps the accusation doesn't so much concern the central function of the Roman Curia as the way of exercising it, since on occasion it seems to override the functions of the bishops.

You mustn't forget the development that has been taking place in the Roman Curia since Vatican II. Today, the Roman Curia is an international body, like the College of Cardinals.

Besides it's now normal for the Holy See to hold frequent consultations with the bishops. The occasions when bishops from all over the world come to Rome to take part in some plenary council or other, in this or that meeting, etc. are more and more numerous. Not to mention the documents issued by the Holy See, which are now usually the fruit of consultation with hundreds of people all over the world.

Do you think that Christian communities should play an active part in the nomination of their bishops?

In point of fact they do already, even though the Church hasn't seen fit to inaugurate a system whereby bishops are elected by the local Churches. When the candidates' names are presented to the Pope, there has already been wide consultation and a vast process of sifting. In this phase, the Bishops' Conferences, individual bishops, and even various priests and members of the laity take part. The Church however has no intention of embracing a system in which pressure exerted by either majority or minority groups might play a not exactly serene role. But already the Holy See now tries to find out about a Christian community's interests and needs, and on this basis then looks for the candidate most suitable for this or that situation. In present circumstances, that bishops should be nominated by the center, after ample local consultation, is one further guarantee of freedom.

Don't you think an Apostolic Nuncio, the man who ultimately forwards the three candidates' names to Rome, might be influenced by pressure groups?

Anything is possible, but the system is such that after presentation by the Nuncio the matter is still not finished. There will be further exchanges between the Congregation for Bishops and the Bishops' Conference. When at last the names are submitted to the Pope, there are sufficient guarantees for one to think that a nomination is not due to a pressure group.

You're aware, I'm sure, that several groups of theologians have criticized the Holy See on this point, maintaining that not a few episcopal nominations in recent years have been at odds with the pastoral policies then in place, at the risk of splitting local Churches into factions. Do you think these criticisms are the product of the aggressiveness you were talking about earlier, or have they some justification in fact?

This isn't a problem that one can discuss in the abstract. In the abstract, one can only say that the Holy See sends a diocese the person most suitable for the situation of that local Church. That in a given situation the Holy See should wish to send someone of solid doctrinal training and proven pastoral experience seems perfectly normal to me. I think, if we were to look at episcopal nominations as a whole, we wouldn't find any pattern of exclusiveness: as though the Holy See were rejecting capable men because they didn't correspond to this or that local Church model. Looking from another angle, you also have to bear in mind that it isn't easy to find candidates for the episcopate. Various factors are at work here: that same shortage of priests; the fact that in many countries only native-born priests can be nominated as bishops, and in the case of young Churches this greatly restricts the possibilities of choice. I might also make the point that very open, revolutionary priests wouldn't make very suitable bishops in present-day conditions, since the people of God in vast majority are not revolutionary. I mean that someone more to the center has a better chance of keeping his diocese united. The first task of any bishop is to be the center of communion and unity. Taking all this into account, I should say that we ought to place our trust in the Holy See and above all in the Pope, where the nomination of bishops is concerned.

Moral theology, a minefield

Doesn't it strike you there's a sort of silence, above all in the moral field, among theologians over tackling the most immediate problems (as for instance the transmission of human life)? Is this because they're afraid of not agreeing with the teachings of the Holy See, or because of the difficulties inherent in these topics?

It doesn't strike me that they are so very silent on these subjects. I mean, the most recent controversies have been, above all, about problems of moral theology. The fact is that in these last decades, moral theology has suddenly found itself in a vortex of new, difficult questions, to which it must try to find answers.

Controversies possibly abound; but don't you think there's a shortage of publications on the more taxing moral topics?

The fact is that we're talking of very delicate questions which still demand a great deal of research, owing to the constant and vertiginous advances in medical science and biological research. And serious research is conducted in reflective silence, not in the hubbub of the press. Furthermore, we mustn't forget that in today's world there's tremendous moral confusion and also a widespread relativism, with the result that norms seem ever frailer to people's consciences. In these conditions, the moral theologian ought to exercise a strong sense of responsibility over the help he gives to the people of God and to the Magisterium. This doesn't mean that he shouldn't intervene publicly; on the contrary, he should, but to clarify, to deepen, to bear witness to the vision of the Gospel and of the Magisterium of the Church as regards the human race and its moral life.

Among those Jesuits involved in moral theology, haven't you ever heard complaints about the lack of opportunity for teaching and publishing freely and with peace of mind?

Everyone working in this field encounters difficulties. It happens because we forget what Ignatius says in the *Spiritual Exercises*: that when a Christian says or writes something we don't agree with, we ought nonetheless to think this is done with a right intention, to serve truth and the Church; we ought not instantly to think he or she is saying or writing something suspect or heretical. These misunderstandings don't normally arise over scientific books or articles, where the authors have adequate opportunity for explaining what they mean; they arise more commonly over short articles or snap interviews, which are indeed the stock in trade of the big circulation newspapers. It's easy, in this second case, to pick on bold phrases or ambiguous arguments, since they are overly condensed, and hold the misrepresented theologian to blame. And perhaps to avoid these dangers is the reason why some of them decide to abandon theologico-moral reflection on the family and human life and devote themselves, for instance, to the ethical bases of commerce or other less perilous sectors. At the same time, when a theologian, be it absolutely unintentionally, sows ambiguities and errors among the faithful, I find it perfectly reasonable for the Magisterium to intervene in order to clarify this or that point, if and when the theologian himself doesn't think he can or should do so. I see the cooperation of everybody as more necessary than ever, if we are to disperse this cloud of nervousness and suspicion that seems to darken the skies of our Christian communities and water down our joy in building the Lord's Church.

No replacements for Rahner and de Lubac

In the past, even in the recent past, the Jesuits enriched the Church with great theologians. Is this happening today? Haven't you somewhat neglected the cultural training of young Jesuits, with the result that fewer illustrious theologians are issuing from your ranks?

I recall it being said at the Extraordinary Synod of Bishops in 1985 that the religious and theological culture of the faithful was dropping off at a worrying rate. There may be many reasons for this but there's no doubt, at least as far as the Western world is concerned, that the fall in the vitality of the Church has also entailed a diminution of theological culture. This is because, in the Society as well as in other religious institutes and in the seminaries, the young arrive by no means so well equipped as regards their religious training as in the past. Add to this that today science is undergoing as it were an explosion, which brings about the predominance of analysis as against synthesis, of specialization as against a global and organic vision. This is true in the field of theology too. Today it gets rarer and rarer to find theologians with a deep and organic knowledge of all theology. Here too specialization predominates: in biblical, or liturgical, or spiritual theology. Sometimes specialization is exclusively concentrated on this or that historical period in the development of the discipline in question.

All this is to say that people like Rahner or de Lubac, who made a synthesis of all theology, aren't likely to find replacements today. Even so, the Society has a number of specialists in the various theological fields, and these often collaborate with the Magisterium in preparing documents or in other ways.

Is it true that over the last twenty years, the number of Jesuits involved in cultural pursuits has dropped, as against those who have preferred to devote themselves to the apostolate, particularly the social apostolate, without first putting in time in lengthy studies?

Certainly the Society, like almost every sector of the Church, has been going through an anti-intellectual period. The result of this has been a sort of instant apostolate. Now, work in the field is important, but the Society has always believed that serious study is needed for the apostolate to be most effective.

Today this tradition of ours has been reinstated in full force, and even those who in the past were keen to commit themselves at top speed to the service of the poor now realize this service can't be rendered merely by being a presence; it demands competence, and hence long preparation in all sorts of fields.

Is collaboration by Jesuits with other religious institutes apparent or real? Doesn't collaboration run into obstacles, such as competition over recruiting new vocations or over occupying certain apostolic fields?

Today, collaboration between religious is real. To give an example, I may say that many religious belonging to other institutes are employed in many of the Society's works, just as there are Jesuits taking part in projects started by other religious Families. For instance, in the *Fe y alegria* popular schools, founded by the Jesuits in Latin America, there are all sorts of religious and members of the laity involved. These forms of collaboration are destined to increase. About competition between religious over recruiting for vocations, I don't think this exists, for the good reason that each religious Family has its own charism, and the Lord is the one who summons the young to sanctify themselves according to this spirituality or that; at most, we try to help young people to identify the type of apostolic life to which the Lord is calling them. As for occupying apostolic fields, we have a directive from Saint Ignatius written into the *Constitutions,* according to which we ought to abandon an undertaking if we see that others are already discharging it well, and devote ourselves to greater needs. We try never to forget that, by virtue of Baptism, we are already children of the catholic, that is to say, universal Church.

The Society and the new movements within the Church

In recent decades the Church has seen the birth of numerous spiritual movements, taking every kind of juridical form: secular institutes, prelatures, fraternities, free associations. What do you think about this flowering?

As a gift of the Spirit, as the Holy Father has said many times and as was hammered home by the Synod of Bishops on the Laity. Certainly the Magisterium, certainly the bishops, have to discern, in concrete cases, whether or not they're dealing with a gift of the Spirit, but there's no doubt, especially in the Western world, that these movements constitute a clear sign of the Church's vitality. We ought to give thanks to the Lord for this gift and try to understand what it is he wants to tell us with these new forms of ecclesial vitality. It seems to me they signify that Christians increasingly want to live the faith communally and that an anonymous, impersonal Church has no power to attract. As in the past when the Spirit of God raised up great spiritual movements to reaffirm various aspects of the faith and the Christian life, which were in danger of being lost, so this is happening now.

What relations does the Society maintain with these movements?

Because of their spirituality and because they are in a certain sense specialists in community life, many religious Families collaborate with these movements to some degree. So it is with the Jesuits. Obviously we have a special relationship with those movements which are based on Ignatian spirituality, as for instance the Communities of Christian Life (formerly Marian Congregations). The relationship is one of spiritual affinity, not a juridical one. And then, many Jesuits have contacts through helping or collaborating with new groups and movements: charismatic, neo-catechumenal, etc.

Don't you find these relationships rather strange: between the religious of an Order characterized by intellectual discipline and, say, a movement, such as the Charismatic one, in which the emotions apparently hold sway?

I don't accept the antithesis between reason and emotion. It's true the *Spiritual Exercises,* forming the basis of the Society's spirituality, don't lack for rational elements and some people say the intellectual part is dominant, but the *Exercises* rely very much on the heart as well, ending with an important meditation on how to live the love of God. Ignatius wants to exploit the emotions so as to make them too a vehicle for the Lord's voice. So I don't think it strange that Jesuits should have very good relations with the charismatic movements. There's another reason too why movements of this sort are to be encouraged: they are the Catholic response to the fundamentalist sects. You see, it is a fact that since Vatican II the Latin Catholic Church has become somewhat cold, at least in its liturgy. It has certainly been right to get rid of unhistorical elements and over-emotional and pietistic incrustations, but there was perhaps a need, in some way or other, to fill the void thus being created, to find other forms capable of expressing those emotions which inevitably accompany religious activity. I think these movements are discovering the new forms we need. Of course, always with the proviso that the manifestation of the Spirit is not to be confused with mere emotion for emotion's sake. Discernment on the part of the Church's pastors will be needed for this, but equally necessary would be a revitalization, particularly of the Latin liturgy, by means of powerful symbolic actions.

Don't you think some of these movements, and I'm thinking particularly of the charismatic ones with their emphasis on the extraordinary elements of the faith (healings, speaking with tongues), are more likely to alienate our contemporaries from, rather than attract them to, the Church?

All I'm saying is that, if the Church can't offer people an opportunity to express their pathos, no one should be surprised if pathological manifestations then occur on the margins of the Church or outside it. The Church has the ability to tackle this problem effectively, since in the course of a long history it has come to embrace every dimension of human nature. Can you possibly imagine a Church without a spirituality of the heart, with its biblical origins and its devotion to the Heart of Jesus? For example, there's considerable opposition to pilgrimages nowadays, but people still want to go on pilgrimage. You could see this in August 1989 at Santiago de Compostela, where more than four hundred thousand young people went on pilgrimage with the Pope. Many pilgrimages, those to the Holy Land for instance, can be a sort of spiritual exercises and are certainly a wonderful opportunity for catechesis.

You say these movements are the Catholic response to the fundamentalist sects. Isn't there a danger of their becoming sects themselves within the Church?

This was discussed very frankly at the Synod of Bishops on the laity, and the movements were warned not to become exclusive and to remember they form part of a Church in which there are charisms of many kinds, no one of which is absolute.

Relations with Opus Dei

People often talk of the less than cordial relations between the Society of Jesus and Opus Dei. Is this gossip or hard fact?

It's only gossip, constantly nourished by the press. It's probably due to the fact that when Opus Dei was started, in Spain, there were certain difficulties with the Jesuits; also because the political climate was very tense. As for today, I must say my relations with the Prelate of Opus Dei are very cordial and when difficulties arise we boldly tackle them together. However, relations between the Society and Opus Dei cannot be frequent and constant since our respective missions within the Church are different.

Generally speaking, how is collaboration between Jesuits and the Catholic laity?

Growing fast. In all our works, from universities to retreat houses for Spiritual Exercises and the parishes, the number of lay-people taking part in our apostolic labors is on the increase. I might indeed say that many of our works couldn't go on without this growing cooperation from the laity.

How do you see the Church of the next decades? More on the sidelines or more at the center of human society? As yeast in the dough, or rather as a fortress secure in its own certainties?

With Ignatius, I reply: The Lord has given the Church Peter and Paul: Peter to confirm his brothers in the faith, Paul with a mission to evangelize the world. Between them, they express the Church. You can't imagine a Church occupied in looking solely after Christians, in building a protective citadel round them; nor can you imagine it only as yeast or as the grain that has to die, in such a way that no one could any longer see where the Church is. They are two partial visions that have to be synthesized, so as truly to correspond to the Lord's will.

10

COMMITTED TO THE PRESENT, WITNESSING TO THE FUTURE

The position of religious in the Church

Many investigations and much publicity are being devoted to the crises among religious, that is to say, among those Christians who make public profession of the three evangelical counsels of poverty, chastity and obedience. Do you share the diagnosis?

Some people think that religious life is in crisis, whereas others insist that this crisis is itself a sign of normal life and actually of growth. There are difficulties, of course: in some regions the crisis is due to the ageing of the members of the religious institutes; in others it is attributed to the growth of a bourgeois mentality, even making itself felt in the religious life. In any case one fact is indisputable: religious life is searching for its position in a Church undergoing renewal, in a changing world. Religious of either sex are the first to suffer when a local Church becomes divided or finds itself having to live in a critical situation owing to political or social conditions. In spite of this, you have only to travel a little beyond the frontiers of your own country to realize what an immense amount of good religious of both sexes manage to achieve in the difficult conditions of our times.

What is the message religious life is meant to give to the Church and to the world?

I deduce it from the origins of religious life in the Church. In the fourth century the Church, having received legal recognition, settled into a sort of spiritual comfort, no longer living in an environment of persecution and martyrdom. Men and women then arose who perceived God's call and protested against the compromises and pacts of a Christianity happily installed in the fleeting world. In the depths of their being they became aware of the need to testify, for the good of the Church, the City of God-with-us, in which are the true roots of the future people of God. It's in this perspective of denunciation that we need to locate the care manifested by the Spirit of God that the words of Scripture should not remain a dead letter but be embodied in people's lives and transform them. Now, precisely because the Gospel insists on the need for love to manifest itself visibly in works of service to the poor and afflicted, there are men and women in the Church who feel themselves called to be Christ to the needy. Every type of human misery has brought a religious Family to birth within the Church, in answer to that need. The explanation for this is none other than Christ himself, who wills to be helped and served in the poor, as the Gospel reminds us.

Can the eschatological summons, with the radical nature of the commitment, provide an explanation for the difficulties and tensions which not uncommonly arise between religious institutes and the hierarchy of the Church?

Be it said at the outset that religious life doesn't exist for its own but for the Church's sake. It cannot be disputed that the Lord calls each of us in a very personal way, but no one becomes a religious for his or her own good but rather for the holiness of the Church. And this is why it pertains to the Church to pronounce on the authenticity of the gift that is being offered. It is however a fact that Orders and Religious Congregations know the temptation of wanting to monopolize the Spirit of the Lord. In religious life, there is a permanent temptation to situate oneself on the margins of Church life or actually to put oneself above the ordinary condition of God's people. From another angle, there is always a possibility that some members of the hierarchy — as the lives of the founders, Saint Francis and others, prove — may not immediately discern the specific nature of the Spirit's gift. In such a case, as Saint Paul said long ago, there is a risk of extinguishing the Spirit. All this notwithstanding, Ignatius of Loyola was convinced that accidental tensions between the Church hierarchy and religious life cannot build up into permanent conflict: sooner or later it comes about that the Spirit of the Lord is recognized, at work in religious life and in the Church at large. One consequence of the fact that religious life is born by inspiration of the Spirit is that a religious institute cannot be autonomous over deciding when to be born and when to die; it exists completely at the service and at the mercy of the Spirit. The Church alone has received the guarantee that it will last forever. No religious institute has received any such guarantee.

It follows that a religious institute, once its founder's charism is exhausted, once the function for which the Spirit brought it into existence has ceased, should disappear. But who guarantees that its disappearance doesn't depend more on unfaithfulness or adverse historical factors? Or ought these facts to be taken as signs that the original charism is exhausted?

The Passover of the Lord, with its mystery of life and death, is present in all religious foundations. It isn't very surprising that, at a given moment of history, God's people should need a different kind of service of prayer or of charitable works from those already in existence. This is why, even today, we see religious Families being born and dying out. The disappearance of a religious institute doesn't necessarily imply a negative judgment, since a religious Family's future depends less on the personal holiness of its members than on the will of the Spirit of the Lord: to him pertains to use it for the Church's good. All this ought not to lead us too hastily to suppose that the inspiration of the Spirit, which is at the origin of a religious Family, is exhausted. Often there are unsuspected energies within for a renewal.

Since the Second Vatican Council, most religious institutes have attempted to renew themselves. Has this been a genuine effort to recover the original charism or a sociological adaptation to altered historical conditions?

All the meetings and reexaminations, all the discussions and conferences, (probably far too many) held by religious institutes are basically only a manifestation of that availability never to put the last full stop to the commitment to always being ourselves, to always staying as we were founded, by the grace and initiative of the Spirit. And so today, religious life as a whole offers a witness of availability. It isn't a matter of changing our life and work because we itch for change. It isn't a matter either of making certain adjustments merely in response to often very superficial demands: tastes, fashions, or present-day ideologies. No, what matters is to have the evangelical creativity to read the signs of the times by the light of the Lord and within his Church. Only thus can we respond to the call of the Spirit, who makes us feel his prompting in the prayer of discernment. We should be daring enough to accept the Spirit's invitation as the basis of our entire life and activity. A religious Family able to be entirely open to the Spirit of God and to give itself with apostolic enthusiasm will always have the future assured that God wills for it.

Religious life: "sign," not "model"

In days gone by, religious were singled out as specialists in holiness and prayer, and what they had chosen was known as the life of perfection. Can this still be so today, when we see the flowering of lay communities and movements specially given over to prayer and the radical practice of the evangelical counsels?

Our male and female religious certainly don't claim a monopoly on prayer and holiness within the Church. The monks of Egypt were already admitting as something very probable that this or that mother of a family in Alexandria was much holier than all the specialists in asceticism and prayer there might be there among them in the desert. The Second Vatican Council then put an end to all pretensions of this sort by reminding us that we are all called to holiness. We cannot conceive of the Gospel as divided into two compartments: the first with requirements for the laity; the second with demands exclusively for the religious. The Lord invites us all to pray unceasingly and calls all to be perfect as the Father who is in heaven is perfect (cf. Mt 5:58).

How then is the particular call of religious to be defined?

To put what the Second Vatican Council attributes specifically to religious into very simple words, I should say that our specific commitment is to follow the Lord more nearly. And this is why religious can be a sign capable of effective influence on other members of the Church, so that they can bravely and wholeheartedly discharge the duties required of their respective Christian vocations.

But can following the Lord more closely depend on juridical or sociological status? I mean, why should living in a certain manner recognized by the Church automatically entail greater nearness to Christ?

The Second Vatican Council, I recall, had great difficulty in defining religious life owing to objections of that sort. The most important reason is that religious life is a gift of the Spirit, and the Spirit will not suffer himself to be defined. Because of this, religious life exists in surprising diversity. The Council did however say that the monopoly of holiness doesn't lie with religious, since all the faithful are called to the fulness of Christian life and holiness. It thus becomes very hard to spot the difference between the ideal of holiness for every Christian and the one for religious. Certainly the difference isn't conferred by juridical or sociological status, but rather by an existential condition. That is to say, when we use the expression to follow the Lord more closely, we are referring to the lives of the Apostles, who likewise existentially followed the Lord. Among them, there were people whose holiness might have been in doubt, and one of them was actually a traitor; yet, for twenty-four hours in the day they stood with the Lord; and the Lord it was who determined their way of life. Today, in one way or another, religious do the same; they lay their lives out totally in the service of the Lord, in accordance with the various needs of the Church and the human race.

Isn't it rather odd, from a pedagogical point of view, that religious should be singled out as the model of Christian life, when they live in conditions very different from those of 99 percent of Christians?

Religious life isn't a model of Christian life, of holiness or of charity; rather, it is a sign. Not only are religious men and women as such not better than their brothers and sisters in Christ, but neither does the religious vocation mean that it is the only model or most perfect realization of the Gospel. In other words, the important thing is not that religious should be imitated but that they should be perceived as a sign that God's people have no abiding city here on earth but are journeying towards the City that is to be. In the heat of the struggle for justice, we run the risk of forgetting what is essential. Hence the need for that sign, given by the Spirit, to illuminate and point out the paschal path, which is the only road for humanity's full salvation. Rather than a solution, religious life is a reminder of the Gospel, offered to those who are seeking the City of God. Constantly religious life reminds God's people of the meaning of their existence, of their paschal journey — to the presence of the Risen One — towards new heavens and a new earth.

The ecclesial significance of religious vows

We haven't yet spoken about what distinguishes religious externally, that is to say, the public profession of the evangelical counsels through the vows of poverty, chastity and obedience. What is the meaning of the vow of poverty?

This has to be understood in the context of society and the Church. In the next few years, we shall probably experience an even more accentuated and accelerated economic development than we are experiencing today. Under the prompting of the Spirit, religious are being called to assume — more than we are already doing — the beatitude of the poor. This involves living like them, with them and among them. And this is not only to remind us that the good news is contrary to the immense interest in getting and hoarding the goods of this world, but also and above all so that we shall put on the Lord Jesus and make his feelings ours, by remembering that, though he was rich, he became poor so that we should become rich by proclaiming his Word and by sharing in his Body and Blood. To give a voice to those in this world who have no voice presupposes a life which is not of this world and which refuses to consider the present world as the last word. And this, because now we are already living in hope of the Savior who is to come.

This witness may be effective in a prosperous world. Is it also effective in poorer countries where the vast majority of people live in even greater poverty than the religious?

This is undoubtedly a serious difficulty. It often happens that religious living in Africa, Asia, Latin America and other parts of the world where there are many poor people, hear people say: "Your ideal of poverty may be all very well for Europe and North America, where the people are rich; but it certainly doesn't go down well with us, because we live in poverty and have got to get out of it." Here the problem hinges on the meaning of the word poverty, which is used for such extremely varied situations that even the expression "vow of poverty" can give rise to misunderstandings. To try to explain, let me remind you that even in conditions of extreme poverty, to be poor of heart is not an automatic fact. It's possible to be rich of heart in penurious conditions; this is when we think exclusively about ourselves, completely forgetting about other people. Contrariwise, the poverty of Christ is to be understood primarily as solidarity: indeed he who was rich became poor to make us rich. In other terms, the purpose of evangelical poverty is not penury, against which we rightly protest, but stripping ourselves of selfishness, to make ourselves open to others and to God. When Jesus says: Woe to the rich! he does so because he condemns their selfishness, their inaccessibility to others, their self-sufficiency. People who are rich of heart try to get their hands on everything and then not share; this is the opposite of life in God, which is communion with the Trinity and saving love for our fellow beings. The poor are the image of God, not because they own nothing but because they are usually open to one another, sharing the little they have with one another; in a word they are in communion with one another. The religious vow of poverty is meant to prompt us into this communion with others; and hence all that religious possess ought to be shared with others. If this is how it really is, it doesn't matter if religious have fine, efficient works; what matters is if they embody a spirit of sharing. We shouldn't have an ideology of poverty but bear witness to that freedom from material goods that characterized the life of Jesus. The Lord Jesus was not only the first person to say: Blessed are you, the poor! but was and still is the first and truly poor man in the Kingdom of God.

Let's pass on to the vow of chastity. What is the message of this vow for the world today?

From its origins until now, religious life has never existed as a way of life in the married state. That is an eloquent sign in itself. Furthermore the City of God-with-us is proclaimed and prefigured and the new commandment is existentially lived, in that community whether of brothers or sisters, which is not born either of blood or of the flesh, or of human will, but of God. It isn't the rejection of human sexuality or the flight from the responsibility, implicit in Christian married love, of coping with a family. It is a sign that the personal love of Christ can satisfy human love when it is called to this vocation in religious life. Lastly, it is a powerful eschatological sign, since by renouncing the opportunity of perpetuating ourselves by having children, we are existentially confessing that everlasting life in the Risen Lord which will never fail.

And what is the ecclesial significance of the vow of obedience?

By means of obedience, and within their ecclesial and communitarian works of mercy, religious manifest one of the fundamental aspects of their vocation. They are genuine apostles, not because they exercise an apostolate, but because they try to live like the Apostles. They follow Christ in service and communion, and this they do in accordance with the teachings of the Gospel and of the Church founded by the Lord. In other words, they renounce leading a life of their own, setting up their own home, having a profession of their own, and allow themselves to be guided, by obedience, into forming part of an apostolic body which follows the inspiration of the Spirit of the Lord, giving primacy to the will of God and relocating the vital space of their personal freedom in God.

This is the theologico-spiritual substance of the vow of obedience. How do you actually put it into practice?

If the vow of chastity, which consists in consecrating the most intimate aspect of ourselves to the Lord, depends less on the cultural context, the opposite is true for the vows of poverty and obedience. The vow of poverty depends very largely on the economics of the era. Similarly the way of living the vow of obedience depends on the structure of human society. It also depends on the differing traditions of the various religious Families: there are indeed those that are eminently democratic, as is the case with the Mendicant Orders (Franciscans and Dominicans) and those on the other hand that are monarchical, like the Society of Jesus. Let me stress however that these categories ("monarchy," "democracy") are applied here, as in any other ecclesial context, in a merely analogical sense. The heart of the matter is that, regardless of the social structures of the day, religious try to live, again by virtue of the vow of obedience, as a community of brothers or sisters, as the case may be.

In the Society of Jesus, has the way of living the vow of obedience been altered in recent times?

When, a little while ago, I wrote a letter to the Jesuits about communal apostolic discernment, someone immediately informed the press that the Society was going democratic and clearly conveyed the impression that our Order had been an absolute monarchy. In fact, of course, discernment has its origin in Saint Ignatius himself who intended the superior to engage in ample consultation before making a decision.

How different is this from what happens in civil society, where directors and managers normally consult with all sorts of people before arriving at a decision?

The difference is marked, since in the Society the aim of consultation is to discover, as well as one can, what God's will is.

Furthermore, in the Society, everyone comes in order to obey and no one has come in order to command; the only one to command is the Lord. So, rather than of powers of command, one should talk of ability to listen, so as accurately to find out what the Lord wants of us.

Religious life in human society

You've concentrated mainly on the ecclesial and eschatological meaning of religious vows. Do you think they still have a social significance, a message for the society of today?

The witness of consecrated chastity, lived in a morally permissive environment, the proclamation of a poverty that rejects the values of a consumer society, apostolic obedience proclaimed in an environment critical of any form of authority: these taken altogether provide an extremely powerful witness, especially in the societies of the wealthier countries.

Only a witness of contradiction?

Not only: if by contradiction you mean merely to deny or reject the existing state of affairs. The witness religious wish to give is aimed at safeguarding the values of society. So, chastity in religious life helps to safeguard Christian married love, and this can't be done without sacrifice; religious poverty likewise proposes to safeguard the well-being of all if founded on justice; our obedience helps to safeguard the freedom of all, inasmuch as it is based on the response to God's call, and not on human coercion.

You said: "Especially in the societies of the wealthier countries." What about the poor ones?

In Third World countries, religious life is a prophetic sign, accusing a world of entrenched power and wealth which will not bother about its poor brothers and sisters. But as a sign, religious life goes further still. From the depths of its consecration, sincerely lived in commitment to the poor, it proclaims that only the poverty lived by Christ can lead anyone to the unique beatitude: the riches of God. Only a poor person can destroy poverty, struggle for justice, free human beings from slavery and penury. Thus, by means of liberations effected in this world, the religious will proclaim and prepare in tangible form that perfect liberation consisting in the Kingdom of God which is to come.

Since the liberations achieved by religious in this world have the force of symbol rather than of fact, isn't there a danger that the proclamation of a perfect liberation in the future will be a modern version of that resignation preached to the poor in days gone by?

Certainly not. Meanwhile you must agree that even the best society we succeed in constructing still won't be the Kingdom of God. But this wouldn't be a reason for giving up and not doing anything to improve the society in which we live. All our projects, all our commitments, have to be signs of liberation, all the while knowing that true liberation comes from God and is of God. It's a difficult concept for someone to accept who takes an immanentist view of human life and history but it's the dialectic of the Christian life: we have to give ourselves to do the best we can, knowing however that, in the end, we are unprofitable servants, and that it won't be we, for all our efforts, who will build the Kingdom of God, but that this same Kingdom will be given to us as a gift, as the loving gift of the Father, the Son and the Holy Spirit.

The contrary objection is that the commitment of religious to the poor risks becoming pure philanthropy, thus obscuring the eschatological sense of their consecration. Would you agree?

No. Religious Families usually occupy themselves with poor people who are of little interest to other organizations and ideologies. Furthermore, religious very often lend a voice to those who cannot express themselves, precisely because no one is brave enough to speak up on behalf of those who wield no clout in society and are forced to keep quiet. In other words, religious life's commitment to the poor for the coming Kingdom's sake is marked by the gratuity of Christ's love. The Lord gives himself without reserve and exacts no return for his giving of himself to others. This is the spirit in which religious try to perform their service. And it's precisely this free-giving of the gift — of one self, of one's own material and spiritual goods, of one's own time, etc. — that characterizes religious life as a sign of the Kingdom of God, as a reminder in the here-and-now of God's fullness and transcendence.

11

AN EXACTING TRAINING
FOR ARDUOUS TASKS

Birth of a vocation

You entered the Society of Jesus when you were very young. What made you choose this Order?

I didn't join the Society all that quickly. In the Low Countries in those days, anyone planning to enter a seminary or religious institute attended "classical high school." I, however, not as yet having heard the call to the religious life, went to "scientific high school" and only when that was over did I decide to join the Society. Before being sent to the Novitiate, I had to put in an extra year learning Latin and Greek.

What made you decide to join the Jesuits?

The call came in the way the Lord normally uses: through the coincidences of life and personal contacts. I was living in a parish served by the Dominicans, where there was a very robust liturgical life. The Dominican ideal — *contemplata aliis tradere* — appealed to me and attracted me very much, but in the end I chose the ideal of the Jesuits who ran the college where I was studying — *contemplativus in actione* — since I was much attracted by the Society's missionary zeal.

What are the principal stages in the training of a Jesuit?

In the old days, the candidate went straight into the Novitiate, for the good reason that the Society didn't have minor seminaries of its own. Today, this is gradually changing, especially in those countries where the general religious and theological culture is somewhat impoverished. So we now demand a period of preparation of our candidates, for them to acquire those elements of religious training they will need for coping with the Novitiate. At the same time, the candidate's maturity of character is also taken into account. The Novitiate then begins; this lasts for two years and is firmly geared to Ignatian spirituality as mediated through the *Spiritual Exercises* and the *Constitutions* of the Society. The aim of the Novitiate is to assimilate the Ignatian spirit and to personalize one's call within the Society.

Does the Novitiate begin with a month of Spiritual Exercises?

No. The first year is devoted to general preparation, comprising various aspects of spirituality: the Bible, theology, various forms of prayer. Also, during this period, the novice is trained to live in community. The novice makes the *Spiritual Exercises* for a month during the first year, but not at the beginning.

What happens during the second year of the Novitiate?

In the second year, it's a matter of putting the spirituality of the *Spiritual Exercises* into practice and during this period the novice also makes a thorough study of our *Constitutions*. At the same time as this, apostolic experiments take place, which are designed to reveal the qualities and gifts that the candidate can put at the Church's disposal, through the Society. I don't mean extraordinary ones, you understand, but practical ones which have relevance for the Jesuit life: helping with the sick, getting to know the poor, contacts with the world of the young. One experiment, which has undergone some degree of modification, is that of pilgrimage, which forms part of our tradition; this of course goes back to Ignatius, who had been a pilgrim and always thought of himself as being one. Rather than to a shrine, today the Jesuit novice is sent as a pilgrim to environments where there is no strong or explicit Church presence, and there he lives for a week or two, trying to bear witness to the Word of God.

After the Novitiate, what's the next stage in the training of a Jesuit?

First of all, there's the first religious profession, which binds the candidate but not the Society. That is to say, the young religious isn't yet completely a part of the apostolic body of the Society. He promises to bind himself to it, commits himself to it for his whole lifetime, and in this sense the vows he pronounces are perpetual ones, but he is kept waiting, the better to understand what God's will is regarding him. As long as the training lasts, the Society doesn't consider a Jesuit to be completely a member, since during this period he may discover that his true call lies elsewhere. Full integration into the Society occurs with final vows at the end of a further long period of training.

The period of studies

Tell me about the stages of this later period. After first religious profession, what does the young Jesuit do next?

In the old days, there was the Juniorate, during which the young religious studied one or more languages and was trained, even literarily, to expound the Word of God in public, either by preaching or in writing. After a period of not having the Juniorate, we have now reinstated it, having seen the need, besides that of language study, of learning how to express oneself properly in public, especially in an age like ours dominated by the mass media. The Juniorate usually lasts for a year but is fairly elastic and depends on how well prepared in these fields each scholastic is; there are some who need two years, some only one, and some who can skip this stage altogether. The next phase is devoted to learning about the world to which we are being sent as apostles. This is the period of philosophy. Before Vatican II, three years were devoted to pretty deep study of the great problems afflicting the human race and of the principal philosophic systems. Subsequently, changes were introduced, suggested by various factors: developments in philosophy itself, the vast progress of the social sciences, changes in university programs. For a certain time, our scholastics studied the social sciences and major authors more, and systematic philosophy less. Today, the balance is being redressed and philosophy as such is back in pride of place.

This part of a Jesuit's training lasts for three years, even today?

Two or three years, depending on the scholastic and university systems.

The Juniorate and two or three years of philosophy apply to all Jesuits being trained. Does this go for lay brothers too?

The Juniorate, yes. Lay brothers devote the subsequent period to their own subject of specialization, and this may involve an infinite range of possibilities from medicine to engineering, from hydraulics to the arts. Philosophy is really for those Jesuits who feel themselves called to be priests.

For these, do their theological studies begin right after their philosophical ones?

No, there's a period known as regency, during which most trainees work in one of the Society's undertakings, so as to take their first steps in the apostolic life. This is useful for those — and there are more and more of them — who already have a degree or a doctorate in this or that field. For the rest, it's the time for non-theological university studies. This phase lasts two or more years, depending on the type of studies chosen and on the level at which one begins. For me, studying linguistics while working in one of our colleges, this period lasted four years.

So a Jesuit student who wants to become a priest comes to his theological studies quite late in the day. How many years does theology take?

For theology, we have to stick to the programs laid down by the Holy See. The Society however insists that its clergy should at least graduate in theology, and that means not less than five years of study.

Priests when over thirty

Totting up the years, it's hard to imagine a Jesuit being ordained to the priesthood until he's well into his thirties. Aren't you being too exacting, given the shortage of clergy the Church is suffering today?

The Society's tendency not to rush the ordination of its clerics to the priesthood is conditioned by our apostolic commitment, and this requires very thorough preparation. And it's been the tradition of the Society, from the days of Ignatius himself, not to think of the period of studies as something separate from the true apostolic life; it already is the apostolate. It's a truth we have above all to remind the young of, for they tend towards the instant apostolate and don't much appreciate whatever takes a long time to pay off. Ignatius experienced the same temptation and when still a layman administered the *Spiritual Exercises* with great success, but he came to realize that to make valid and durable contributions there had to be more investment in preparation. Furthermore, it's true in theory and in experience that one can

only give what one has first received. I'm convinced of that, even
with regard to the Third World, where it's easier to listen to
objections to the waste of such a long training, when the poor are
suffering and in urgent need of our ministrations. For my part, I
think the Third World needs thoroughly trained helpers precisely
because the problems it has to struggle with are so fearfully
serious and complex.

*Having reached the age of thirty or more, the Jesuit cleric is
ordained a priest. Is his training finished then?*

No, for he still isn't really and truly a Jesuit. After a few years
of pastoral work or specialized studies, he will have to do a third
year's Novitiate, which includes another month of *Spiritual Exercises*. Only then, with personality sufficiently mature and a
knowledge of the problems awaiting him, can he freely say his yes
to the Lord and pronounce his final religious vows; at which point
he is a Jesuit in every respect and the bonds with the Society are
reciprocal.

*It's certainly a long, hard training. Isn't it also a bit discourag-
ing for the young men of today who tend, as you say, to want to get
involved in the apostolate right away?*

It's true, some young men are put off by the thought of such
an exacting training and, though very sympathetic to us, do not
join the Society. This however may be a sign that the Lord is not
calling them to be Jesuits. And yet it is also true that not a few
young men understand the importance for the Church not only of
an exacting cultural training as such but also of the thoroughness
of the studies in preparation for particular apostolic tasks.

*Did Vatican II produce changes in the methods by which
Jesuits are trained?*

It introduced new perspectives. The first is inculturation.
Unquestionably today we are more careful to foster a greater

sensitivity in Jesuits to the problems of local Churches, without in any way derogating by this from the universality of our mission. A Jesuit joins the Society of Jesus, not this or that Province, and this entails his availability to work in any part of the world. The second perspective is personal responsibility for studies but this, rather than being an innovation, is a rediscovery of Ignatius, who wished Jesuits not to be walking encyclopaedias but men who managed to assimilate knowledge to such degree as for it to be an efficacious apostolic tool; today we should say we wanted witnesses, not loud-speakers. In this connection, problems inherent in the way university studies are organized sometimes arise where the syllabuses are so crowded that they don't allow any depth of personal involvement. Now, what doesn't become part of one is easily lost or at any rate makes no impression.

Assessment of candidates

In assessing candidates' personal maturity for the religious life in the Society, do you ever have recourse to the psychological sciences?

That's not a general criterion of the Society; it depends rather on the culture, on the country. It's a known fact, for instance, that in the United States, recourse to the psychological sciences is now a part of daily life, and so it is quite common in that country even for candidates for the religious life to ask the opinion of the psychologist before they take the final plunge. Anyhow, it's fairly normal now for novice masters to have a nodding acquaintance with the psychological sciences as part of their cultural baggage — without claiming to be psychologists or to turn novitiates into psychotherapy centers. That would lead to distortion of religious life and of vocation itself, which is born from the experience of God.

What sort of young man asks to join the Society? Youths who dream of doing something exceptional for the Church? Young men who think to find a rigorous environment for some sort of intellectual work? Young men who want to be strictly guided in their spiritual life?

The young men who ask to become Jesuits are generally attracted by our apostolic ideal, which is to be contemplatives in action, that is to say, men who wish to lead a life of union with Christ and at the same time to spend themselves in the service of their fellow human beings. They are attracted by the missionary spirit characterizing the Society and by the competent service that we aim to give the Church. All this is conveyed by our witness. I mean to say that these characteristics are not plucked out of the air by the young men but are perceived through the witness borne by Jesuits joyously living their vocations.

Do some young men join the Society in order to flee from the world rather than to prepare themselves for evangelizing it?

Flight from the world might be the opportunity for discovering one's true vocation. Were it the only motivation, the candidate wouldn't be able to persevere. A young man who isn't mature enough to get married and shoulder responsibility for a family isn't likely, humanly speaking, to last long in the Society, where a sense of responsibility not less than that for a family is required. It's during the *Spiritual Exercises* however that the novice examines himself in depth before God and purifies the motives behind his own vocation.

In comparison with the past, what is your novices' perseverance quotient?

I don't have the statistics from memory, but I can say that it's harder to persevere today than it used to be, since today the young are not so likely to encounter exemplars of perseverance, whether in marriage, or in religious life, or even in the priesthood. It then happens that, out of honesty, young men may not enter religious life, thinking it impossible for them to be able to commit themselves forever.

The apostolate dictates the destination

How does the cultural specialization of young Jesuits come about? Does the choice of university studies take account of the inclinations of the man in question, or of the needs of the apostolate?

I'm not trying to avoid the question if I say that both factors are taken into account. The criterion that guides us is that if the Lord sends us this or that young man with his gifts, this is so that these may be cultivated and put to use in apostolic service. Not only this: we all have to listen, since God speaks to all. Saint Benedict used to say it was a good rule for the abbot to listen even to the youngest of his monks since the Lord might well speak through the mouth of the youngest. Certainly, in the case of a choice having to be made between a candidate's inclinations and the needs of the apostolate, the former will carry the day, since personal gifts are given to us for the Kingdom of God.

In your case, was it your choice to specialize in linguistics?

In my case, the criterion was applied that I have just been describing. The superiors knew I had a certain facility for languages and asked me to specialize in linguistics, which I was very happy to do. Then I went on cultivating this particular field for twenty years as professor of general linguistics at the University of Beirut.

Having been attracted by the Society's missionary spirit, you ended up as professor of a pretty dry science like linguistics. Where's the apostolic ingredient in all this?

First of all, let's clear the ground of a fairly common misapprehension: that of supposing that apostolic commitment is only expressed in work that is strictly pastoral. This is not so. Any work can become apostolic. Furthermore, in certain multiconfessional situations, contacts between Christians and other believers (Moslems for instance) are possible only through educational institutions. And here we're talking about those deep, personal contacts in which we don't set about converting the other person — for it is the Lord who works conversions — but in which it is natural to explain the tenets of one's own faith.

Is the Jesuit's apostolic destiny the fruit of choice, of dialogue, or of obedience?

We always say it's the fruit of a discernment. The Superior and the subject together seek that which the Lord truly wills. Hence it's not some individualistic thing, it isn't the choice of my future. It's dialogue, but not in the sense that a compromise is sought between the positions of the Superior and those of his Jesuit brother. It's best put as obedience to the Lord through the Superior, who is trying not to let his own ideas prevail, but the apostolic good. This is the normal way of doing things. In certain cases, affecting for instance China, the USSR, Japan, we ask for volunteers. Here we are dealing with peculiar situations from the political or cultural point of view, and these require special vocations. Similarly, all Jesuits know the Churches of Africa are always in need of help, and many men offer themselves for this apostolate. Another apostolic field, for which the Society has been asked to make its members available, is aid for refugees throughout the world. This is an apostolate to which more than one hundred Jesuits are committed.

In the Society, do you have times of recycling, sabbatical periods for redirecting one's religious and apostolic choice?

Evaluation of what we are doing is one of the most characteristic features of Ignatian spirituality. This habitual attitude apart, every year we make the *Spiritual Exercises,* which certainly provide an opportunity for reorienting one's own apostolic choices. Every Province, besides, promotes, particularly during the summer, meetings and gatherings for cultural and theological renewal. There are also your real and actual recycling initiatives, with special premises for these. For instance, at San Leopoldo in Brazil, there's a house which accepts Latin American Jesuits who, at least once in their lives, want to take time off to take stock. This consists of a month of *Spiritual Exercises* and study sessions on the new documents of the Church, on the renewal of the apostolate, on everything conducive to progress. The same thing happens here in Rome, at the General Curia, where every year hundreds of courses are held on Ignatian spirituality. These are courses beginning or ending with the *Spiritual Exercises,* lasting for eight days or for a month, in the Holy Land. I think I can safely say that the urgent need for reorientation is widely felt in the Society as being an integral part of the Ignatian charism.

APPENDIX
CHRONOLOGY OF
THE SOCIETY OF JESUS

15th century

1491   Birth of Ignatius of Loyola at Azpeitia, Guipzcoa (Spanish
            Basque country).

16th century

1521   Ignatius wounded at the siege of Pamplona.
1522   Ignatius' retreat at Manresa.
1523   Pilgrimage to the Holy Land.
1524   Ignatius a student at Barcelona.
1526-27   Student of philosophy and theology at Alcalà.
1527-1535   Student in Paris.
1534   The vow of Montmartre.
1537   Ignatius ordained priest in Venice.
1538   The first ten pre-Jesuits in Rome.
1540   In March, Francis Xavier sent to India. On September 27, Paul III
            approves the Society of Jesus.
1548   In Messina, the Society opens its first college for non-Jesuit pupils.
1549   Francis Xavier arrives in Japan. First Jesuits in Brazil.
1551   Opening in Rome of a free school of letters, the germ of the
            future Gregorian.
1556   Death of Ignatius.
1556-65   Generalate of Father Diego Laínez; Jesuits spread to Germany,
            Austria, Hungary, Egypt.
1565-72   Generalate of Saint Francis Borgia; the Society established in
            Poland, Lithuania, Peru and Mexico.
1583   Matteo Ricci in China.
1584   Consecration of the Church of the Gesù, in Rome.

17th century

601	Matteo Ricci in Peking.
1606	Roberto Nobili in India.
1609	Beginning of the "Reductions of Paraguay."
1615	Peter Claver among the negro slaves in Colombia.
1627	The first Jesuit in Tonkin (modern Vietnam).
1656	Pascal publishes the *Provincial Letters*.

18th century

1704	Pope Clement XI forbids "Chinese rites."
1759	The Jesuits hounded out of Portugal and its Asiatic colonies, and from Brazil.
1764	Dissolved by law in France.
1767	The Society expelled from the Spanish dominions (America and the Philippines).
1773	On August 13, Clement XIV suppresses the Society.
1775	On November 24, Lorenzo Ricci, former Superior General of the Jesuits, dies a prisoner in Castel Sant'Angelo.

19th century

1814	Pope Pius VII restores the Society.
1834-54	Scores of Jesuit foundations in Europe, Latin America and Asia.
1846-47	Vincenzo Gioberti writes *Il Gesuita Moderno* (The Modern Jesuit), five volumes of rabid polemic against the Jesuits, whom he accuses of obscurantism.
1850	In Naples, first appearance of *Civiltà Cattolica*.
1872	Chancellor Bismarck's laws against the Jesuits.

20th century

1907	Pius X's encyclical *Pascendi* against Modernism: Jesuit publications side with the Pope and conduct a fierce controversy with the ex-Jesuit George Tyrrell, one of the leading exponents of Modernism.
1909	Foundation of the Pontifical Biblical Institute, entrusted to the Jesuits.
1930	Inception of Vatican Radio, entrusted to the Jesuits (first director, Father Giuseppe Gianfranceschi).

1950	Encyclical *Humani generis* of Pius XII against the new theology and scientific theories threatening to encroach on Catholic dogma. The theologians de Lubac and Daniélou give up teaching in Lyon-Fourvière and Paris respectively. Father Teilhard de Chardin is transferred to New York (where he dies in 1955).
1950	In Milan, the review *Aggiornamenti sociali* first published.
1965	31st General Congregation of the Society: Father Pedro Arrupe elected Superior General of the Jesuits.
1975	32nd General Congregation: tension between the Society and Paul VI.
1981	Illness of Father Arrupe. John Paul II nominates Father Paolo Dezza as his delegate for the Society.
1983	33rd General Congregation: Father Peter-Hans Kolvenbach succeeds Father Arrupe.